all about PEER PRESSURE

by GEORGE EAGER

Designed and Illustrated by DIANA PHILBROOK

MAILBOX CLUB BOOKS • Valdosta, Georgia

Copyright ©1994 George B. Eager
Published by: **Mailbox Club Books**
        404 Eager Road
        Valdosta, Georgia 31602
        Fax (912) 245-8977

Library of Congress Catalog Card Number: 93-80759

Paperback   ISBN 1-879224-13-5
Hardback   ISBN 1-879224-17-8

CONTENTS

Chapter 1

I WANT TO BELONG

Peer pressure is powerful . . .

awesomely powerful. The urge to belong . . . to win the approval and acceptance of others.

Even when you become part of the most popular group in school, sometimes it doesn't last. Like what happened to Trey.

Tonight my football team, the Lytle Pirates, won the district championship. Since this is my senior year, nothing could be more exciting to me. I can just feel the electricity in the air.

Right now the whole team is out having a good time—gettin' rowdy. As a member of the Lytle Pirates, I should be out with them, having the time of my life. But I'm not. Earlier this evening I looked down at the cast on my broken foot and thought, You know, since I haven't been able to play for the last five games, I've been more or less ostracized by the rest of the team.

I noticed it even at the pep rally this afternoon. The band started playing the school song, sig-naling all the seniors out onto the gym floor. Of

I want to belong!

course, I went out with the rest. The football players were on one side hugging each other and singing—forming their own private huddle. The cheerleaders were grabbing the better players. I was sort of left out. I felt embarrassed being in front of three hundred students with my senior class, and standing behind the huddle.

So I edged up close to my

football friends and tried to bring up an old
private joke. They laughed for a second and then
got back to their private huddle. Suddenly I
began to see what it feels like not to be a part of
the most popular group in school.

These are supposed to be my friends. They are
the school's in-crowd. I have struggled through
football just to be a part of this group. Now I am
punted out. Why? Just because I hurt my leg.

Trey had worked hard to get into the fast lane of the
team. He practiced. He sweated. He "clean and jerked"
tons of weights. For what? To belong. To be in the
most popular group. In the in-crowd. But now he was
out. Dumped.

NEW KID IN TOWN

You're a freshman. Or you've just switched schools.
You're sitting at home, in your room, staring at your
poster of U2. What if the kids at this school don't like
U2? you think to yourself. What if the kids at this new
school don't like me? Your anxieties keep you awake.
Through the Late Show, through the Late, Late Show,
through Morning Exercises with Francis Fitness. You
wonder, over and over: Will I fit in anywhere?

So did Mike.

The summer before I started high school I had a
lot of fears about making friends. And that's why
I got involved with Ed's group.

Ed, who lives down the street, was my first
"real" high-school friend. At that time he was
going to be a junior and I, the soon-to-be fresh-
man, looked up to him. I was willing to do just
about anything to be a part of Ed's group. So
that summer Ed gave me an education about his
definition of fun times—and an education about
his understanding of friendship.

Ed's idea of a good time with friends was

8

sitting around smoking marijuana. I remember the first night I got stoned. About two houses down from where I live there's a ditch between two houses. Ed and I went back there and he showed me a bong filled with Sprite. We lit up.

That was just the beginning. As the summer went on I was stoned more than I was together. We smoked up every day. When school started in the fall, we kept right on smoking. We were wasted most of the time, so a lot of the things I did during this time are pretty fuzzy.

One thing I do remember was stealing. We'd go into grocery stores and drugstores and take junk food and cigarettes. Again, this was Ed's idea of a good time. I was never sure about doing this, but I couldn't refuse. I wanted to fit in with my group of friends.

Mike got caught stealing. He had a couple of cigarette cartons stuck down his pant leg. He was humiliated. All because he wanted to please Ed and his cronies. He'd wasted a summer being wasted. All because he needed that special friendship, that special peer group.

What about Ed? Well, when Mike got caught with the goods, Ed got caught with nothing. Not one smoke. Sure, he pushed Mike into ripping off grocery stores. But when push came to risk—Ed left the hard part to Mike. Some friend. Some great guy. Some peer. Is this what friendship is all about?

MAKING THE GRADE

Dreams. You have dreams of belonging—to that special group. You know it's a good group, one of the best. Your parents even say so. Your friends admire anybody who's in it. It takes a lot of work to get in and stay in. You gotta keep those grades up. You gotta make special meetings and practices. All to get in. All to stay in.

Shannon "got in"—sort of.

I'm a sophomore flag twirler for the MacArthur High School Brahma Bulls. When I joined the team I was really excited.

To explain, let me tell a little about the team and their outfits. Each girl carries a six-foot pole with a white-striped blue banner attached to it. On the end of the triangular-shaped banner is a long silver strip of cloth—which really whips around when you make quick movements. Each twirler wears white boots, royal blue culottes, and a blue-striped white blouse with puffy sleeves. The uniform also has a large satin bow tie. Topping it all off is a white cowboy hat with one side tacked up and a long plume in the band.

It's all very colorful and neat—especially when the flag team is synchronized with the marching band. As a matter of fact, both the band and the flag team won first place last year in state competition.

Added to all of these attractions was the fact that some of my friends from church were twirlers. One of the girls from my youth group was even the colonel—the highest-ranking person on the team. This girl kept telling me how much fun twirling was. It didn't take a lot to convince me. I could hardly think of anything more exciting than being a part of this elite group. The following spring I went out for tryouts and made it.

Then my troubles began. There were thirty-eight of us on the team, but only thirty-two could perform on the football field. The rest served as alternates (a nice term for being stuck on the bench). I was an alternate.

The first couple of games, I wasn't too upset about not performing. But as the season went on, and I didn't get to march, I became more and more discouraged. I even cried during morning practices.

Sure, I wore the uniform, but I still didn't really belong.

GOOD PEER PRESSURE

Not all peer pressure is bad. Peer pressure can be a force for good. Just one person who stands up for what he believes can influence others.

Remember Trey? Before he broke his leg, he had spent a day with David, working in a hay field. The in-crowd called David a "nerd" because he wouldn't party with them. Trey said,

That day, as the perspiration dropped off my chin in a steady stream, I looked at David up there on the hay wagon and I realized I admired him for his guts. He didn't seem to have any desire to be part of the in-crowd. He was his own

11

man. . . . I didn't have David's guts. He refused to drink: I didn't. . . .

After that day with David, my parents caught me drunk. Things got real tough for a while. After things calmed down at home, I had a chance to do a lot of thinking. My time with David helped stimulate that thinking. It wasn't anything that he said that really changed things. It was just his style. He lived out what he felt was right—inside.

I started saying to myself, "Why should I be pushed around by what others think?" . . . I don't want to drink anymore. It's really getting to the point where I don't care what the in-crowd is going to say. . . . I'm just thankful for guys like David. He helped get me thinking right. Just knowing he can stand up for what he believes has given me the courage to do the same. People like him help set the pace for people like me.

What about Mike? Mike had to get another group of friends. He found some friends who really cared about him as a person. Says Mike: "My friends now are real friends, not like Ed. When I need them, they're there. And when they need me, I'm around. It's a two-way kind of friendship."

Sometimes it's not just exceptional individuals, like David, but entire groups who provide positive peer pressure.

Take Shannon, for instance. A group of her friends on the flag team turned out to be true friends. They didn't reject her. They stood by her and encouraged her. She stuck it out because a group of her friends really cared.

Good peer pressure.   ○ ○ ○ ○ ○ ○

From the book, *Peer Pressure*, by
Chris Lutes, ©1987, Campus Life Books

Chapter 2

"I'M SOMEBODY"

Most of the people you see on television are not only physically beautiful, but they are also smart and personable. Many of them are rich. They seem to have everything under control.

Where does that leave the rest of us who don't have all these things? It leaves us feeling inferior—like we came out on the short end of things. We would do well to remember that TV is not the real world. Most people are like us and have the same kind of feelings that we have.

Almost everybody has feelings of inferiority and worthlessness at one time or another, but the "uglies" hit hardest during the teen years. Ask any number of teens if there is anything about themselves that they would like to change. Most all would name at least one or two things. Some would have a whole list.

It has been wisely said that we need the serenity to accept the things we cannot change, courage to change the things we can, and wisdom to know the difference.

There are some things you cannot change. You must accept them. There are other things that you can do something about. You can work on these. Here are some suggestions:

- **Recognize that other people have the same feelings that you have.** When you see your classmates smiling and laughing, you may think that they never have feelings of worthlessness like you have, but that is not so. Everyone has these same feelings at one time or another.

- **Recognize that beauty doesn't make a person happy.** Do you think that beautiful people are the happiest people in life? Well, they aren't. Dr. Martyn Grotjohn, professor of psychiatry at the University of California Medical School, made an exhaustive study of "beautiful people." He wanted to find out how they behave, how they relate to others and how they feel about themselves. He said, "It has been a source of startling surprise to me to see the amount of depression, loneliness, and deep unhappiness among beautiful people."[1]

- **Learn to do something well.** This is one of the best ways to gain confidence. One problem with feeling worthless is that you don't try, and when you don't try, you don't succeed. And you need to succeed at something to make you feel good about yourself.

Find something you like to do and work at it. Make the most of what you have. Develop a skill that will make you feel good about yourself.

- **Avoid drugs.** Avoid drugs and alcohol like you would a pit bulldog with AIDS! Those who don't feel good about themselves often take this route, but it's a dead end. You don't need that garbage. It only makes things worse, and it will destroy you.

- **Make friends.** You do not have to be beautiful or smart or have a lot of money to make friends. The best way to have a good friend is to be a good friend. Show special attention to those who have difficulty making friends. Respect them and accept them as they are. They will love and appreciate you for this. Nothing helps your self-confidence like having good friends that love and appreciate you.

Things that happen on the outside do have an effect on us, but what changes us most is what happens on the inside. You can change the way you think about yourself. You can say, "I am a unique, one-of-a-kind person. There has never been another person exactly like me and there never will be. I'm somebody! I'm priceless!" Changing the way you think about yourself can change your life. The story of Johnny Lingo and his "eight-cow wife" brings this out beautifully.

JOHNNY LINGO'S EIGHT-COW WIFE [2]

Patricia McGerr

When I sailed to Kiniwata, an island in the Pacific, I took along a notebook. After I got back it was filled with descriptions of flora and fauna, native customs and costumes. But the only note that still interests me is the one that says: "Johnny Lingo gave eight cows to Sarita's father." And I don't need to have it in writing. I'm reminded of it every time I see a woman belittling her husband or a wife withering under her husband's scorn. I want to say to them, "You should know why Johnny Lingo paid eight cows for his wife."

Johnny Lingo wasn't exactly his name. But that's what Shenkin, the manager of the guest house on Kiniwata, called him. Shenkin was from Chicago and had a habit of Americanizing the names of the islanders. But Johnny was mentioned by many people in many connections. If I wanted to spend a few days on the neighboring island of Nurabandi, Johnny Lingo could put me up. If I wanted to fish, he could show me where the biting was best. If it was pearls I sought, he would bring me the best buys. The people of Kiniwata all spoke highly of Johnny Lingo. Yet when they spoke they smiled, and the smiles were slightly mocking.

"Get Johnny Lingo to help you find what you want and let him do the bargaining," advised Shenkin. "Johnny knows how to make a deal."

"Johnny Lingo!" A boy seated nearby hooted the name and rocked with laughter.

"What goes on?" I demanded. "Everybody tells me to get in touch with Johnny Lingo and then breaks up. Let me in on the joke."

"Oh, the people like to laugh," Shenkin said, shrugging. "Johnny's the brightest, the strongest young man in the islands. And for his age, the richest."

"But if he's all you say, what is there to laugh about?"

"Only one thing. Five months ago, at fall festival, Johnny came to Kiniwata and found himself a wife. He paid her father eight cows!"

I knew enough about island customs to be impressed. Two or three cows would buy a fair-to-middling wife, four or five a highly satisfactory one.

"Good Lord!" I said. "Eight cows! She must have beauty that takes your breath away."

"She's not ugly," he conceded, and smiled a little. "But the kindest could only call Sarita plain. Sam Karoo, her father, was afraid she'd be left on his hands."

"But then he got eight cows for her? Isn't that extraordinary?"

"Never been paid before."

"Yet you call Johnny's wife plain?"

"I said it would be kindness to call her plain. She was skinny. She walked with her shoulders hunched and her head ducked. She was scared of her own shadow."

"Well," I said, "I guess there's just no accounting for love."

"True enough," agreed the man. "And that's why the villagers grin when they talk about Johnny. They get special satisfaction from the fact that the sharpest trader in the islands was bested by dull old Sam Karoo."

"But how?"

"No one knows and everyone wonders. All the cousins were urging Sam to ask for three cows and hold out for two until he was sure Johnny'd pay only one. Then Johnny came to Sam Karoo and said, 'Father of Sarita, I offer eight cows for your daughter.'"

"Eight cows," I murmured. "I'd like to meet this Johnny Lingo."

I wanted fish. I wanted pearls. So the next afternoon I beached my boat at Nurabandi. And I noticed as I asked directions to Johnny's house that his name brought no sly smile to the lips of his fellow Nurabandians. And when I met the slim, serious young man, when he welcomed me with grace to his home, I was glad that from his own people he had respect unmingled with mockery. We sat in his house and talked. Then he asked, "You come here from Kiniwata?"

"Yes."

"They speak of me on that island?"

"They say there's nothing I might want that you can't help me get."

He smiled gently. "My wife is from Kiniwata."

"Yes, I know."

"They speak of her?"

"A little."

"What do they say?"

"Why, just...." The question caught me off balance. "They told me you were married at festival time."

"Nothing more?" The curve of his eyebrows told me he knew there had to be more.

"They also say the marriage settlement was eight cows." I paused. "They wonder why."

"They ask that?" His eyes lighted with pleasure. "Everyone in Kiniwata knows about the eight cows?"

I nodded.

"And in Nurabandi everyone knows it too." His chest expanded with satisfaction.

"Always and forever, when they speak of marriage settlements, it will be remembered that Johnny Lingo paid eight cows for Sarita."

So that's the answer, I thought: vanity.

And then I saw her. I watched her enter the room to place flowers on the table. She stood still a moment to smile at the young man beside me. Then she went swiftly out again. She was the most beautiful woman I have ever seen. The lift of her shoulders, the tilt of her chin, the sparkle of her eyes all spelled a pride to which no one could deny her the right.

I turned back to Johnny Lingo and found him looking at me.

"You admire her?" he murmured.

"She...she's glorious. But she's not Sarita from Kiniwata," I said.

"There's only one Sarita. Perhaps she does not look the way they say she looked in Kiniwata."

"She doesn't. I heard she was homely. They all make fun of you because you let yourself be cheated by Sam Karoo."

"You think eight cows were too many?" A smile slid over his lips.

"No. But how can she be so different?"

"Do you ever think," he asked, "what it must mean to a woman to know that her husband has settled on the lowest price for which she can be bought? And then later, when the women talk, they boast of what their husbands paid for them. One says four cows, another maybe six. How does she feel, the woman who was sold for one or two? This could not happen to my Sarita."

"Then you did this just to make your wife happy?"

"I wanted Sarita to be happy, yes. But I wanted more than that. You say she is different. This is true. Many things can change a woman. Things that happen inside, things that happen outside. But the thing that matters most is what she thinks about herself. In Kiniwata, Sarita believed she was worth nothing. Now she knows she is worth more than any other woman in the islands."

"Then you wanted—"

"I wanted to marry Sarita. I loved her and no other woman."

"But—" I was close to understanding.

"But," he finished softly, "I wanted an eight-cow wife."

TO SUMMARIZE...

Changing the way you think about yourself can change your life.

Chapter 3

PEER PRESSURE:
FRIEND OR ENEMY?

○ ○ ○ ○ ○   ○

Jeff, who just came in from baseball practice, sits down at the dinner table with his family. The phone rings. It's Ron, Jeff's best friend. "Jeff, I know you just got home, but I need your help with today's math assignment right now," Ron says.

"I can't," Jeff says. "I'm eating. And after dinner I need to work on my research paper that's due tomorrow."

Peer Pressure

FRIEND OR ENEMY?

"But, Jeff, this is the **only** time I can do it," Ron pleads. "Please, I can't do it without you."

Jeff finally gives in and drives to Ron's house without finishing his dinner. A week later, Jeff angrily looks at his graded research paper. He knows it would've been two grades higher if he'd stayed home that night.[1]

It isn't easy to say no to your friends.

In the area of guy-girl relationships, teens are pressured, ridiculed, and talked into doing what they really don't want to do. One girl expressed it like this: "The peer pressure to have sex is incredible! If people find out that you're a virgin, they treat you like the biggest geek in the world. And yet if you're not, they look at you like you're a tramp. You can't win!"[2]

What is "peer pressure?" Why is it so powerful? How do you handle it?

Peer pressure is the pressure you feel from your friends and associates to do things that please them. It causes young people to do things they do not really want to do in order to be accepted by their friends.

Why is peer pressure so powerful? It is powerful because of the need and desire of teens to win the approval of others. Deep down inside, most young people are unsure of themselves. They don't really feel good about themselves. They want others to like them and accept them. That's why they cave in to peer pressure.

An example of the power of peer pressure is illustrated

in a study of teenagers conducted by Ruth W. Berenda.[3] She and her associates brought ten teens into a room and told them that they were going to study their visual perception.

To test their ability, the researchers held up cards on which three lines were drawn. The lines, marked A, B, and C, were of different lengths. Line A was the longest on some cards, while lines B and C were longer on others. As the cards were held up before the class, the researcher would point to lines A, B, and C consecutively, asking the students to raise their hands when the pointer was directed to the longest line.

The instructions were simple and were repeated: "Raise your hand when we point to the longest line." What one student didn't know, however, was that the other nine had been brought in early and told to vote for the *second* longest line. The purpose was to test the effect of group pressure on that lone individual.

The experiment began with the nine teenagers voting for the wrong line. The poor guy who did not know what was going on glanced around, frowned, and then slipped up his hand somewhat reluctantly. The instructions were repeated and the next card was raised. Again, the nine teens voted for the second longest line. Again, the

**Peer pressure
is powerful!**

poor guy who wasn't in on what they were doing reluctantly held up his hand. He didn't want to be the odd ball in the group. Time after time, he sat there saying that a shorter line was longer than the long line because he lacked the courage to go against the other nine, even though he knew that they were, wrong.

You may be thinking, "That guy was just stupid. Most people wouldn't do that." Would you believe that 75 percent of those tested responded in the very same way. Peer pressure is powerful!

Peer pressure seems to be a friend at first because it makes us feel good about ourselves. But in the end it turns out to be a false friend because it leads us to do things we would not do otherwise. When we are in trouble, our "friend" is nowhere to be found. Shari Beardslee of Caro, Michigan, expressed this well in an essay written when she was a high school junior:

He appears to be a loyal friend. He never leaves our side. He helps us meet new friends. He makes us popular. He shows us new ways to enjoy life. He teaches us new hobbies. He shows us how to look cool and how to act like an adult. He makes us feel important. When we're with him, we're never sad or depressed. He teaches us how to get away from everything.

For a while, we're sure no one could ever replace him. He's the best friend we've ever had.

After some time, the fun wears off. He's no longer great to be with. He has changed our whole life, turned us against our parents. We're never with the family. Our other friends have turned away because we are trying to be to them what he has been to us.

He seems to get us into so much trouble. We must always take the blame for the messes he gets us into. Instead of our best friend, he is now our worst enemy.

But by now, it's too late. Our wonderful friend has gotten us into the worst mess of our life, and we can't get out. We regret the day we became friends with this master of disguises. His name? Peer pressure.

Maybe you would like to make good grades and do well in school. But in your crowd, it's just not the popular thing to do, so you mess around like everybody else. In your senior year you decide that you want to be a doctor, but you make a sad discovery. Your grades are not good enough. Guess who is going to make a change in career plans—YOU.

You're a virgin but your friends pressure and ridicule you until you decide to have sex with the next person who asks you. On your first encounter you contract genital herpes. Guess who is going to suffer with this for the rest of his/her life—YOU.

You don't really want to do drugs, but your friends make it very difficult to say no. Before long, you are hooked. Guess who is going to pay the price for this—YOU.

You go to a party with your friends in your car. Your friends talk you into drinking. Later they assure you that it's O.K. for you to drive. On the way home you are involved in a serious accident in which someone is killed. Guess who goes to jail—YOU. And guess who is going to face the court and the judge Monday morning—YOU!

When you stop and think about it, you realize that there is nothing stupid about right-doing, and there's nothing smart about wrong-doing. If something is wrong, it's wrong, no matter how many people are doing it. Like Shari said, peer pressure can get you into big trouble, but you are the one who has to pay for your mistakes.

If *you* are the one who is going to pay, then isn't it reasonable that *you* should be the one to make the choices and not your friends? Think of it like saying yes to yourself instead of saying yes to peer pressure.

The remedy for peer pressure is to stand up for *your* right to choose what *you* will do. We see people demanding their rights all the time. You have rights, too!

You have the right to be yourself. You are a unique one-of-a-kind individual and you have the right to make your own decisions. Nobody has the right to pressure you to do something you don't want to do. If you do things you don't really want to do just to please others, sooner or later, you will be a very confused and a very angry person.

You have the right to have your values respected. The values you establish in your life are important to you. If others have different values, that's their business. But they don't have any right to make fun of you or to try to destroy your values.

You have the right to go out with those who treat you as the very special person you are—those who do not tempt you to do things you know are wrong.

You have the right to care for and protect your body. Your body is your own personal possession and you are going to have to live with it the rest of your life. If others want to do things that destroy their bodies, again, that's their business. But they don't have any right to pressure you to do something you don't want to do.

You have the right to establish and protect your reputation. You have the right to act in a way that makes you proud of your actions, not ashamed of them. You have the right to refuse cheap experiences that degrade you and lower your self-respect.

You have the right to be free from guilt and fear. You can be free from the fear of pregnancy, free from the fear of AIDS and the other sexually transmitted diseases, free of guilt and regret by simply refusing to get involved in sex before marriage. You have the right to do this.

27

You have the right to plan for a happy, satisfying marriage. You have the right to keep yourself for the one you will meet some day—the one you will want to spend your life with.

You have the right to say no. It isn't easy to say no to your friends when they dare you to do something or threaten you if you don't do it. But saying no will help you gain confidence and feel good about yourself. Here are some ways to say no:

- Say, " I don't want to do that." Tell your friend that you value the friendship, but that you just don't want to do that.
- Say, "My dad (or my mother) would kill me if I did that." Don't be afraid to use the strictness of your parents to turn down a dare.
- Say, "I'm proud to be a good red-blooded American chicken, and I expect to live longer because of it." Use humor to lighten the situation.
- Say, "No, thanks. I need all the brain cells I've got!" to refuse drugs and alcohol.
- Say, "No, thanks. See you later," and leave quickly.
- Say, "I promised myself I wouldn't do that, and I believe in keeping my word."
- Say, "Sorry, but I've got to go." Then get lost.
- Say, "No" in a firm voice. If you have to, simply repeat your answer. Don't give any excuses. Just calmly keep saying no. If the pressure continues, end the conversation and leave.

TO SUMMARIZE...

Peer pressure is the pressure you feel from your friends and associates to do things that please them. You have the right to say no to peer pressure and make your own choices. If somebody tries to twist your arm, say no. Feel good about taking charge of your life!

Chapter 4

WHAT ABOUT SEX?

○○○○○ ○

what about SEX?

When young people talk about the choice to become sexually active, they are often counseled, "Wait until you are ready. If you don't feel that you are ready, don't do it, but if you feel that you're ready, then it's okay."

Ready for what?

Ready to throw away your priceless virginity?

Ready to make a conquest?

Ready to be another notch in some guy's belt?

Ready to feel like a tramp?

Ready to bring a new life into the world?

Ready to get a sexually-transmitted disease?

Ready for AIDS?

WHAT IS SEX LIKE?

What is sex like? It depends on the circumstances. In a marriage where there is love, commitment and tenderness, it is a beautiful and awesome experience.

31

Outside of marriage, it can be cheap and unsatisfying.

Many young people say, "What's so great about sex? I tried it and it was no big deal."

The reason why it was "no big deal" is that there was no real love, no commitment, and no security which are so vital to a satisfying sexual experience. One girl described her first sexual experience like this:

"It was awful. I was so scared. I didn't feel any thrill at all. I kept thinking, 'What if someone should drive up and see us?' Within a few minutes I was putting on my blouse and hating myself for throwing away something precious on a guy who didn't care about me—and one I didn't care about either."

WHY SHOULD I SAY NO?

One of the questions most frequently put to counselors by young people is this: "What do YOU think about having sex before marriage?"

What they want to know is this: "Are there any good reasons for saying no to sex before marriage? If so, I'd like to know about them."

There are plenty of good reasons for saying no to sex before marriage. They can be summed up in this statement: *What you get out of it is not worth what you stand to lose by it.*

Whether you use a condom or not, if you are sexually active, there is a good chance of pregnancy. Some people think having a baby is like having a wonderful doll to love—one that you can put on the shelf when you're tired of playing with it. But that's not the way it is. A girl wrote,

I am 17 and already my life is messed up. Ted and I went steady for six months and we began to do things we had no right to do. I became pregnant.

We both quit school and got married right away. My folks thought it would be best if we moved out of town, so we did. I hate my life and

what I have done to Ted. The baby cries all the time and gets on Ted's nerves. He drinks too much, and I can't blame him.

We live in a dump, and there is no money for sitters or movies or decent clothes. Ted never says anything, but I know he must hate me because I got him into this. I'm afraid he hates the baby, too. He never holds her or pays attention to her.

There are times when I think this is all a bad dream, and I'll wake up at home in my own bed, and get dressed and go to school with the kids I liked so much. But I know too well that those days are over for me, and I am stuck. I'm not writing for advice. It's too late for that. I'm just writing in the hope that you will print this letter for the benefit of other teenagers who think they know it all—like I did. [1]

DON'T LET AN STD CATCH YOU!

Another good reason for saying no to sex before marriage is the danger of getting a sexually-transmitted disease (an STD).

A recent study indicates that as many as 56 million Americans have a sexually transmitted disease. There are 12 million new cases each year. On an average, every day 8,219 teenagers are infected with an STD for the first time. Every day, 2,740 people, mostly teenage girls, are infected with the HPV virus which causes genital warts. [2]

Statistics are important, but they don't tell the full story. If you happen to be one of the teenage girls getting genital warts, you can expect hard, fleshy bumps to appear within three months after exposure to the HPV virus. They appear around the vagina, but they can show up well inside the vagina or the cervix, making it difficult to detect them.

Doctors can usually remove the warts by freezing,

burning, chemical solutions or, when necessary, surgery. But who wants that? Furthermore, treatment does not eliminate the virus. Genital warts can come back. Genital warts have other very serious consequences. Some types of genital warts have been linked with cancer of the cervix. Any woman who has ever had genital warts should have a Pap smear every year to check for signs of cancer.

Some people have the virus and do not have warts. But they are carriers of the disease just the same and can pass it on to their sexual partners. The virus can cause cancer of the penis. Condoms do not provide protection against this virus.

Another sexually-transmitted disease that you don't want to get is genital herpes. Every year anywhere from 200,000 to 500,000 people get herpes. This disease is highly contagious. One contact with it, and you've got it for life.

Herpes won't kill you but it sure can mess up your life. Here's a first-hand account of what it is like to live with genital herpes. This guy got it from one encounter with a girl when he was a teenager.

I've got herpes.

There's nothing I can do about it. It's with me for life. A lifetime of pain and shame for a few moments of passion. It won't kill me, but I won't kill it either. . . .

For years I've lived with it. Breakouts on my penis (like cold sores of the mouth, but much more painful and irritating). With herpes you get a lot of extras. Like isolation, fear of others finding out about it, and not knowing when you will get an attack, embarrassment, low self-esteem, contemplation of suicide, stress like you wouldn't believe, and bitterness. Add to that the fear of having to tell the girl you want to marry, fear of her getting it, fear of the children getting it at birth.

I didn't want to give it to somebody else, so I just didn't date girls for a long time. And if I did, I just never let myself get into a potential sexual situation.

Why am I risking the embarrassment of digging up my past and present hurts to share them with you? For one reason. So you won't trade in a beautiful gift (your gift of sex to your marriage partner on your honeymoon) for an unmeaningful, stained sexual experience.

I was lucky, you could say. After many years I met a girl I really liked. She liked me too. We began seeing more and more of each other. Love began to grow for both of us. I wanted to ask her to marry me, but my terrible secret hung over me like a cloud. I had to tell her. It was the hardest thing I have ever had to do. What if she rejected me? I couldn't blame her if she did.

With fear, trembling and much tears, I shared it with her. Fortunately, she loved me enough to want to go ahead with our plans, so now we're engaged. But we still will have to live with it the rest of our lives. I'll still have the fear of her getting it or the children getting it at birth.

If only I had waited until my honeymoon night. If only my parents had warned me. If only my school had taught me. But I can't blame them. I have to be responsible for my own actions. . . .

Part of the pain for herpes patients is the conviction of being damaged goods—the feeling that they are unclean, dirty. One woman said, "We're looking for someone to love. In this world our chances are so slim anyway. Then you add herpes and you think, 'Why should anyone want me now?'"

Many teens think they can go to their doctor and get a quick cure for most anything, but that's not true.

Dr. Robert C. Noble, an infectious-disease expert, said, "The truth is, doctors can't fix most of the things you can catch out there."

A doctor said that one of the saddest things he has to deal with is the numbers of teenage herpes sufferers who come into his office, cry, and say, "No one will ever want to marry me now."

Would you risk a lifetime of regrets for a few moments of pleasure? That's not a good trade.

DON'T CONDOMS PREVENT STDs?

No, they do not *prevent* sexually transmitted diseases. They *reduce* the risk of getting an STD, but they don't *eliminate the risk*. Dr. Noble says, "I'm going to tell my daughters that having sex is dangerous, and condoms give a false sense of security. *Reducing* the risk is not the same as *eliminating* the risk."

Condoms are not even foolproof in preventing pregnancy. They can and do fail 15.7 percent of the time annually in preventing pregnancy.[3] A study among unmarried, minority women showed a failure rate of 36.3 percent annually.[4] If a girl is sexually active, the question she must ask herself is not, 'What would I do *if* I got pregnant?' Instead, she should ask, 'What will I do **when** I get pregnant?'"

Depending on condoms to prevent AIDS or other sexually-transmitted diseases is much, much riskier. A woman can get pregnant only two or three days in a month, but STDs can be transmitted 365 days in the year. If condoms are not used properly, or they slip or break just once, deadly viruses and bacteria can be exchanged. Only one mishap is all it takes.

In a study of three clinics in Brooklyn, N.Y., 21 percent of the female patients with STDs said that condoms were used regularly. [5]

In an article in *The Los Angeles Times*, Dr. Steven Sainsbury says,

My 15-year-old patient lay quietly on the gurney as I asked the standard questions: "Are you sexually active?" She said, "Yes." Next question: "Are you using any form of birth control?" The response was "No." Next question: "What about condoms?" Response, "No."

Her answers didn't surprise me. She had a rip-roaring case of gonorrhea. It could easily have been AIDS. I treat teenagers like this one every day. Most are sexually active. Condoms are rarely used and sporadically.

Yet in the midst of the AIDS epidemic, I continue to hear condoms touted as the solution to HIV transmission. The message is: Condoms equal safe sex.

As a physician, I wish it were true. It isn't. It is a dangerous lie. . . .

Condoms fail frequently due to improper storage, handling and usage. The breakage rate during vaginal intercourse is 14 percent.

*For condoms to be the answer to AIDS, they must be used every time, and they can never break or leak. So what's the answer? The only answer is no sex until one is ready to commit to a monogamous relationship. The key words are **abstinence** and **monogamy**.*

Dr. Noble says, "We should stop kidding ourselves. There is no safe sex. If the condom breaks, you may die."

AIDS: DON'T GET IT!

Of all the sexually-transmitted diseases, AIDS is the most feared. With good reason, too. If you get AIDS, you die. It's just that simple.

In the weeks after Magic Johnson announced that he had the AIDS virus, young people in this country reacted first with shock, then with concern. But that lasted only a few weeks. Then, it was back to risky business as usual.

The number of cases of AIDS among teens doubles every 14 months. You may not know any teenagers who have full-blown AIDS, but don't let that fool you. "There aren't many teenagers who have full-blown AIDS," says Dr. Robert Johnson, a specialist in adolescent medicine. "But that's only because it takes the disease a long time to develop."

"What you should know," says Dr. Johnson, "is that many young adults who have AIDS probably were infected with the HIV virus during their teenage years. They got sick from the disease two or three, or even 10 years later." [6]

That's one thing that makes AIDS so dangerous. A few weeks after becoming infected with the HIV virus, a person may have an initial reaction which may be something like flu. But then the HIV virus goes "underground" and causes no further symptoms for years.

During all this time the infected person may be apparently very healthy, but nevertheless he/she is a carrier of the HIV virus and can infect others *every time they have sex—without knowing that they are carrying the AIDS virus.*

This is one of the most treacherous aspects of this dread disease—that millions of people will infect millions of others, who will in turn infect millions of others, without knowing for years that they have a fatal disease.

"HOW CAN I TELL IF SOMEONE HAS AIDS OR ANOTHER STD?"

You can't! The problem is that 90% of those who have the HIV virus don't even know it themselves. It can be years after a person has HIV before he or she sees some sign of the disease.

However, the moment a person gets the HIV virus,

whether he knows it or not, and even though he doesn't feel sick or have any symptoms, he can give it to others.

Some teens think they can tell if a person has the AIDS virus by looking into their faces, or by what kind of clothes they wear, or whether or not they are a "nice person." *You cannot tell who has the AIDS virus by looking at them.* Not even a doctor can do this.

THE AIDS VIRUS IS INCREDIBLY SMALL

One thing that makes AIDS so deadly is that the HIV virus that causes AIDS is incredibly small. The HIV virus is one twenty-fifth the width of the human sperm.[7] It can easily pass through the tiniest imperfections in surgical gloves . . . or condoms.

Researchers studying surgical gloves made of latex, the same material recommended for use in condoms, found "channels of 5 microns that penetrated the entire length of the glove." [8]

A micron is one millionth of a meter. An imperfection of 5 microns would be about **one-twelfth** the width of one of your hairs. But the HIV virus that causes AIDS is only *one-tenth of a micron!* [9] Like a teacher said, "Fifty AIDS virus could tap dance through a five micron defect holding hands!"

"Fifty AIDS virus could tap dance through a five micron defect holding hands."

The HIV virus is so small that 5,000 HIV's would fit, side by side, in the diameter of the period at the end of this sentence. [10]

A study was made of married people in which one partner was infected with the AIDS virus. Within a year and a half, 17% of the uninfected partners using condoms for protection caught the disease. [11] That's one out of six.

Look at it this way. If you were considering joining a sky diving club, and you were told that the failure rate on parachutes was one out of six, would you jump? Probably not. When it comes to something that is a life or death matter, we don't want to take any unnecessary risk. [12]

At a conference of 800 sexologists some years ago, the question was asked, "Would you trust a thin rubber sheath (a condom) to protect you during intercourse with a known HIV-infected person?" Guess how many hands went up? **Not one!** [13]

IF I'M GOING TO DO IT ANYWAY, SHOULDN'T I USE A CONDOM?

YES, you would be foolish not to. In fact, you should take every precaution possible.

Let's get back to the sky diving club. If the person you loved more than anyone in the world was considering joining this club and both of you knew that the failure rate on parachutes was one out of six, what would you say to your beloved? Check one answer below:

—— *I wish you wouldn't join that club, but if you do, be sure to buckle up your parachute tight before you jump.*

—— ***Don't jump!** I love you too much!*

If you checked the second choice, what about yourself? Are you any less valuable than the one you love?

AREN'T AIDS AND THE STDs A DANGER JUST FOR THOSE WHO "SLEEP AROUND"?

It takes only one exposure to the virus or bacteria to develop a disease. Just that one time that you don't use a condom . . . or you use it incorrectly . . . or the condom is defective. One other thing. AIDS and the

STDs don't care who you are. They just care what you do.

Allison Gertz contracted HIV as a teenager after having sex once with an infected partner. Allison doesn't fit the idea most people have of a person with AIDS. She was attractive and outgoing. She grew up in a wealthy section of New York City. She had loving parents and attended top private schools.

Allison didn't sleep around, had never had a blood transfusion and had never used injection drugs. Nevertheless, in 1988 Allison's doctor announced to her that what she had was AIDS.

Because Ali, as she was known to her friends, was young, attractive, and from a wealthy family, the announcement that she had AIDS created a sensation. A New York Times headline blared out: "How Can This Be? How Can Allison Gertz Have AIDS?"

Ali said that she was infected with the AIDS virus as a teenager. She was a popular, straight-A student, but at 15, she and her friends started hanging around a hip night club. "They weren't very specific about carding people, and I looked older than my age," said Ali. "My friends and I thought we were very sophisticated."

At Studio 54, she met Cort, a club employee about 10 years older than Ali. After a two-year friendship, they decided to have sex. Ali remembered a night of candlelight and romance. "We had decided that this was love," she recalled. "The whole point was to see if it would work."

It didn't. Ali explained that they had sex together only once and then decided to be just friends. Eventually Cort drifted out of her life. . . . Years later she found out that Cort had been bisexual and had died of AIDS. She also found that she had the HIV virus.

After several years, Ali developed AIDS. She was in and out of hospitals for years, fighting a string of illnesses from full-blown AIDS. No one wins that battle.

Ali didn't "sleep around." Just one exposure to AIDS. That's all it took for Ali.[14]

"YOU DON'T WANT TO GET THIS DISEASE!"

Dr. John Dietrich, an infectious-diseases specialist, says, "You don't want to get this disease. It's a terrible, slow and sometimes excruciatingly painful way to die. . . . If there's anything I want to plant firmly in your mind, it's that AIDS is no joke. It's horrible and dehumanizing. I've seen a lot of people die from various illnesses. Believe me, AIDS is by far the worst."[15]

Some people think they will miss out on the fun if they say no to sex before marriage. Sex is not much fun when you're sick or dying. Sex is no fun at all when you're dead.

THE GOOD NEWS

The good news is: If you don't already have AIDS, you don't have to get it. Save sex for marriage, marry someone who has made the same decision, remain faithful to each other and you don't have to worry a second about getting AIDS from sex. Nolan Ryan is one of baseball's all-time heroes, holding or sharing 50 major league or league records. Nolan says,

The most important number in my life is "one." There's one woman in my life. Ruth has been the only girl I ever wanted to be with since I was a teenager. That has never changed. I consider her the best friend I have. . . . You stay married to and sleep with only one person, who does the same, and you are not going to get AIDS through sex.[16]

○ ○ ○ ○ ○ ○

Chapter 5

CHOOSING THE BEST

○○○○○ ○

Choosing the Best

More and more teens are choosing abstinence. What is abstinence? Abstinence is saying no to sex before marriage. If you have already been involved in sex, abstinence is saying no to any further sex until you are married.

Abstinence is not saying no to sex forever. It's postponing sex until you are married so that you can enjoy sex to the fullest—truly safe sex.

EVERYBODY IS *NOT* DOING IT!

According to one survey, the number one reason why teens choose to become sexually active is peer pressure. They think "Everybody's doing it, so I guess I ought to be doing it."

"Everybody" is **NOT** doing it. A report by the Center for Disease Control says that 54.2 percent of high school students have had sexual intercourse, but that only 39.4 percent are currently "sexually active." [1] A girl wrote,

> *Dear Abby: Why is all America laboring under the impression that teenagers are sex-starved animals who will grab any partner they can get? Well, it's not true!*

45

I am an 18-year-old girl who has never had sex. I am considered pretty, I date, I'm friendly and outgoing, and I'm an A-minus student. My friends and I believe we should not have sex until we are married, and there are many of us.

The media play up the cheap and promiscuous among us, which is very unfair. Most teenagers are upright citizens with morals and high standards.

Some who are "doing it" have found out that it's not so great. A girl wrote to Ann Landers complaining that, because she and her friends would not make out, they had no dates. She said, "The fast girls are rushed to death." She sounded like she was envious of them and signed her letter "Fourth Choice."

A girl answered that letter, and her answer was better than anything Ann Landers could have said. Here's her letter:

The letter from "Fourth Choice" hit home. The anti-make-outs were unhappy because they had no dates. They said the fast girls were rushed to death. Well, Ann, I'm one of the fast girls, and I'd like to tell you how it looks from here.

I get asked out every night of the week, and I'm sick of these creeps who want to make out all the time. I am also sick of myself. I'm only 17, and my reputation isn't worth a plugged nickel. My girl friends tell me what they hear about me from their brothers, and of course I deny everything. I know now that nine guys out of ten can't be trusted to keep their mouths shut. Whenever I meet a new fellow I wonder how much he has heard.

Please tell "Fourth Choice" that I wish I could change places with her.

—Too Late For Me [2]

46

YOUR VIRGINITY IS PRICELESS

Whether you realize it or not, your virginity is a priceless gift. You can give it to only one person and you can give it only one time.

Young people say, "Have you lost your virginity?" You don't lose it. You give it away. Many young people give their virginity away carelessly. They give it to the wrong person, at the wrong time, and under the wrong circumstances. A girl wrote:

Take my word for it, girls, sex does not live up to the glowing reports and hype you see in the movies. It's no big deal. In fact, it's pretty darned disappointing. I would have waited. . . had I known what it was going to be like.

I truly regret that my first time was with a guy I didn't care that much about. I am still going out with him which is getting to be a problem. I'd like to end this relationship and date others, but after being so intimate, it's awfully tough.

Since that first night, he expects sex on every date, like we are married or something. Our whole relationship seems to revolve around going to bed. When I don't feel like it we end up in an argument. It's like I owe it to him. I don't think this guy is in love with me, at least he's never said so. I know deep down that I am not in love with him either and this makes me feel sort of cheap.

I realize now that the first time is a very big step in a girl's life. After you've done it, things are never the same. It changes everything.

My advice is, don't be in such a rush. It's a headache and a worry. (Could I be pregnant?) Sex is not for entertainment. It should be a commitment. Be smart and save yourself for someone you wouldn't mind spending the rest of your life with. Sign me,

—Sorry I didn't and wish I could take it back [3]

Whether you are a guy or a girl, the most priceless gift you could give to your mate on your wedding night is your virginity. If you haven't given your virginity away, wouldn't it be wonderful to keep it for the right person, at the right time, under the right circumstances? It's like saying to the one you marry, "I loved you before I even knew you. I loved you enough to keep myself for you."

Wouldn't it be great to be able to say that to the one you marry? And wouldn't it be great to have your beloved say that to you!

REAL LOVE IS WHAT YOU ARE LOOKING FOR

Though they may not realize it, real love is what young people need and what they are really looking for.

It's easy to get confused about love and sex. "Making love" and loving someone are NOT the same thing. "Making love" refers to the act of sex which can be performed without an ounce of real love.

Real love is an inner heart attitude which causes you to want what is best **for the other person!** It has three qualities:

1. **It is unselfish**—it desires what is best for the other person.

2. **It is committed**—it hangs in there.

3. **It involves respect**—respect for yourself and respect for the other person.

A good relationship means really getting to know each other and enjoying being with each other apart from anything physical. It involves trust and good communications—being able to talk things out.

A question on the minds of many guys and girls is: Will sex make our relationship better?

The answer is NO. We have already looked at some of the qualities that are necessary in a good relationship. What does being involved sexually do for these qualities? Does it build respect for yourself or lower it? It lowers it. Does it build respect for the other person or lower it? It lowers it.

Does it increase trust between each other? No. It tends to destroy it. Each thinks, "If he (or she) would do that with me, they would do it with someone else." Does it increase communication? No, it does not. The relationship tends to become more and more physical. Sex becomes the main thing about the relationship.

For a relationship to be good, it must be free from fear, worry, and guilt. Getting involved sexually brings these undesirable qualities into the relationship.

Many guys and girls believe that having sex is the way to find real love, but that's not true. You can have sex in a few minutes, but it takes time to really get to know a person and to build the respect and trust which are so necessary to a good relationship.

Girls are constantly faced with this situation: "My boyfriend is trying to get me to have sex with him. I know I shouldn't, but I don't want to lose him."

Loving someone and giving yourself to them does not mean that they will love you back.

You may **think** that the best way to keep your boyfriend is to let him do what he wants to do, but countless girls have learned by sad experience that it does not work out that way. One girl wrote,

I went steady for seven months with a boy I thought was the most wonderful person in the whole world. I thought I'd always stay decent. After a while we weren't satisfied with just kissing.

He asked me to prove my love. I thought as long as we planned to be married in a few years, what would it matter?

I gave in to him, Abby, and I found out it mattered a lot. He lost all respect for me. He started going with other girls. He even talked

about me to the other boys.

Please print this for all girls to see. Maybe it will help someone who is tempted to prove her love like I did. —Sorry Now [4]

Many a girl can never understand why a guy dropped her after she gave in to him and did what he had been begging her to do. In many cases the reason is simple: for the guy, the thrill is in the chase. After the conquest has been made, he loses interest and moves on to the next challenge. The poor girl is left to pick up the pieces of her life the best way she can.

There is another reason why a guy will drop a girl after she gives in to him. He loses respect for her. He may go on for a while, having sex with her, but she becomes "cheap" in his sight. Later on, he is attracted to another girl with higher standards.

Girls, you need to establish your standards—what you will and will not do—**before** you go out on a date. You need some unbreakable rules—like saying no to sex before marriage, even if it means losing some fellow that you really like.

Be up front and tell your boyfriend straight out, "I really like you, but I have decided to say no to sex before marriage. Some day I'll be married and then sex will be everything it should be, and I don't want to take a chance on messing that up. I think you will like me and respect me more if we don't get involved in sex. Maybe you won't, but I'll have to take that chance."

If you lose a guy after telling him that, you will know that it was sex he wanted—not love.

SHOULD GUYS SAY "NO" TOO?

Yes, they definitely should. Getting involved sexually can destroy a beautiful relationship. Many guys have learned this by experience. One wrote,

I have always been a good student. For a long time I didn't date so I could study. But the girls I was

50

dating told me a lot of things, so I decided to study less and play more. Then I met Sandra. From our first date we liked each other a lot. Then the relationship got more and more physical until we had sex. Both of us were really enjoying ourselves.

One day I woke up and realized how far behind I was in my studies. So I got into the books and quit seeing Sandra for awhile. That hurt her and made her angry. Right in the middle of exams she called to tell me she was pregnant.

All I could think of was how do I get out of this mess? I was scared. It turned out to be a false alarm. We went through hell for three weeks. Our relationship was finished. I realized that I didn't love her. I felt guilty. She was deeply hurt. We wiped each other out, just for the "fun" of sex. [5]

Guys get a lot of bad press because of their aggressiveness at times, but some girls are much more aggressive than the guys.

Some girls have such little respect for themselves that they think nothing of calling up a guy and saying, "I'll be only too happy to **prove** my love for you." Guys, if you get tangled up with a girl like this, be prepared for a lot of regrets and misery.

A wise person is one who can foresee the consequences of his or her actions and acts accordingly.

THE LAW OF PROGRESSION

Guys and girls, if you are ready to begin dating or are already dating, you need to know the five "laws" of guy-girl relationships. These are explained in my book, *Understanding Your Sex Drive.* One of these five "laws" is "The Law of Progression." You need to know how this "law" operates.

Most guys and girls want to do what is best for themselves. They have no intention of going all the

51

way, but many of them end up doing it anyway. Why? Because they did not know about the Law of Progression.

What is the Law of Progression? It is this: When a guy and a girl spend time alone together, the relationship tends to move steadily toward greater physical intimacy.

The first physical contact in a guy-girl relationship is usually holding hands. This feels great. Then comes the first kiss. This can send a guy into orbit. Then comes "French kissing"—kissing with your mouth open.

Then comes prolonged sessions of kissing and hugging. Next the hands get into the act. Petting really

the law of PROGRESSION

Being together & Holding Hands

Simple Good Night Kiss

Prolonged Kissing

Start of Relationship

arouses a guy and a girl. In marriage, this is the foreplay that prepares the couple for sex. But your body doesn't know that you are not married. The signal to your body is: Get ready for sexual intercourse.

Once a couple has sex, that marks the end of the relationship as it once was. The physical side of things is now overpowering. After this, every time the couple gets alone, the tendency will be to go all the way. This puts a tremendous pressure on the relationship and sooner or later, it usually results in breaking up.

The best way to deal with the Law of Progression is to cool things on the physical side. You can have a good relationship without getting physical.

Many a girl allows things to start too fast. Before long she and her boyfriend are too far along the path of

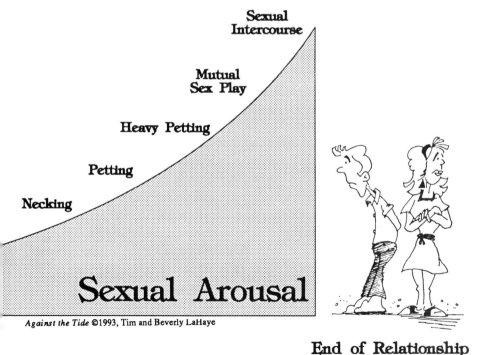

Against the Tide ©1993, Tim and Beverly LaHaye

physical intimacy. She might like to stop and keep things where they are, but the Law of Progression is steadily working and the relationship moves more and more toward sexual intercourse.

MAKING LOVE DOESN'T
MAKE THEM LOVE YOU

Write this in concrete: **Making love with someone does not make that person love you.** You can learn this two ways: (1) by somebody else's experience or (2) by your own experience. You are a lot better off if you learn it by somebody else's experience.

Here is a letter from a girl who learned it the hard way.

Dear Ann: I am a 17-year-old girl, and I want to send a message to other teen-age girls. I have fallen victim to my own stupidity twice now.

A lot of girls use sex to try to keep a boy interested. Why do we do this when all our lives we are told by our parents, church and school that it's wrong? I guess virginity seems old-fashioned in the '90s. But I have learned that some things never go out of style.

In both my relationships, I can look back and see that before sex entered the picture, we laughed more, talked more and went to a lot more places. Once you cross that line, it's all the guys want to do.

Boys don't respect girls who put out. If a guy decides to break up, it won't make any difference whether you've had sex or not. If you use sex to try to hold on to him, that will be the only part of you he's interested in.

Learn to say, "This is as far as we're going," and stick to it before you go too far.

—FEELING USED AGAIN IN OREGON [6]

SAYING NO IS CHOOSING
THE BEST FOR YOURSELF

In a survey of over 11,000 teens, 94% of the girls and 76% of the guys said that it is acceptable to say no to sex before marriage. [7] Teens on a 15-member *USA TODAY's* Teen Panel said that the idea of saving sex for marriage makes sense. Suzanne Linkous, 16, said, "You're not a geek if you are a virgin." Added Eddie Pailen, "A lot of people are not ashamed to be virgins. And if they come across like they are virgins, people don't mess with them." [8]

True love will wait. It's not just okay to say no: it's choosing the best for yourself!

- Like not having to worry about pregnancy.

- Like knowing you're not going to get an STD or AIDS.

- Like having respect for yourself and feeling good about yourself.

- Like being in control of your life and making plans for your future.

- Like being able to tell the one you marry, "I loved you before I knew you. I loved you enough to keep myself just for you."

It is possible to wait . . . and someday you will be glad you did. As the author of this book, I want to share some letters from three friends of mine who chose to say no to sex before marriage. They're not nerds! They are nice-looking, out-going young people just like you.

If you could talk with them, I'm sure you would want to ask them some questions. Why did you choose to not "do it"? How did you manage to remain a virgin? What did the other kids think of you? Are you glad you made the choice that you did? I'll let Kelly, Marya and Shep answer your questions.

"SEX, TO ME, IS TO BE A BEAUTIFUL AND AWESOME THING. . ."

As a high school student I played on the varsity tennis team, was an officer in clubs and was in a high school sorority. Many of my classmates were involved with drugs and alcohol. However, I chose to take a different path.

Now a 21-year-old junior at a large university, I am still not sexually active and do not drink. I am in a sorority and am involved on my campus. I have a boyfriend of three years and he not only respects me for waiting for marriage, he wants to wait also.

While in college, I have heard many excuses people give for having sex, like "It's the natural thing to do," "We love each other," "We're going to get married anyway," and, "Everybody's doing it." (Sorry, but I don't want to be just everybody.) Well, these lines are great, but I have made enough mistakes close to sex to know it was not made to play around with!

Sex, to me, is to be a beautiful and awesome thing created to finalize lifelong commitment and intimacy with that ONE person I want to spend the rest of my life with. I am not going to do anything with a guy that I wouldn't want a girl to do with my future husband.

Sincerely,

Kelly

P.S. As for peer pressure, people naturally want what they can't have. They may tease you about your virginity, but it's probably because they wish they still had theirs.

56

WHY DID I CHOOSE NOT TO "DO IT"?

I am 18 years old and I just graduated from high school. I'm not writing to ask for advice or to tell you about a problem I have.

Maybe my story is not that exciting at all. I always read stories in books about teens who have made mistakes with sex or have tried it for the experience. I know there must be some people who are not "doing it." I know that because I'm one of those people.

When some people find out I'm a virgin at 18 they are shocked. Maybe they are shocked because these days guys think girls who are virgins must be unattractive or unpopular or uninterested in sex.

Maybe I'm not the most beautiful girl in the world, but I am a normal person. I was a cheerleader and my high school's Homecoming Queen. I enjoy dating and plan to enjoy sex one day with the man I marry.

Why did I choose to not "do it"? Well, I have three reasons.

1. I have seen how sex before marriage can ruin a relationship.

2. I think sex is a very intimate, personal thing that I'm not ready to share with just anyone.

3. Having sex will mean giving myself totally to someone. It is a gift so valuable that I want to give it only to the person with whom I will share the rest of my life.

Maybe my letter will help girls like me (and guys) to hang in there and not give in just because their friends do. Sign me,

Marya

"I'M 22 AND I'VE MET THE GIRL I'M GOING TO MARRY."

I'm a normal guy. As long as I have known about sex, I've had a strong desire to try it, but I chose not to.

Someone asked me recently how I had remained a virgin all my life. "I don't really know," I replied. That seemed like the truth to me at the time. Later, as I thought about it, I realized that there must have been something definite to keep me from having sex.

Then it dawned on me. At home I had been taught that sex was to be saved for marriage. I believed that. It had become a part of me.

Sure, I wanted people to like me, but I was not ashamed of what I believed.

If people ever gave me a hard time (which they seldom ever did), I tried not to let it bother me. I knew I was standing up for what I believed was right.

Now I'm 22 and I've met the girl that I'm going to marry. She, too, is a virgin, and I am more glad now than ever that I stayed away from premarital sex. It's about the best move I ever made.

Shep

Chapter 6

TEST YOURSELF !

○○○○○ ○

Test Yourself !

Do you think you know every-thing about alcohol, tobacco, other mind-altering drugs and steroids? Take this quiz and find out.

1 Nobody dies from doing co-caine just one time. **True/False**

2 I don't need to worry about becoming addicted to alcohol or other drugs since I only party on weekends.   **True/False**

3 Because drinking alcohol can make you feel happy, it can't be a depressant.   **True/False**

4 You can get bad acne and go prematurely bald if you take steroids.   **True/False**

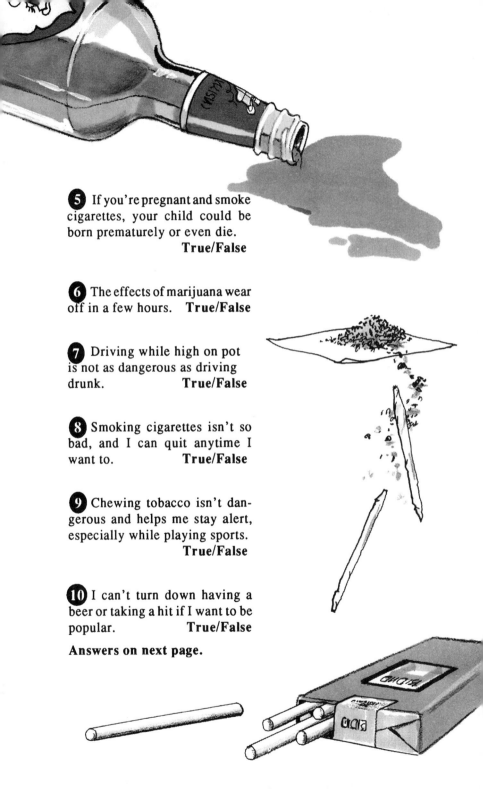

5 If you're pregnant and smoke cigarettes, your child could be born prematurely or even die.
True/False

6 The effects of marijuana wear off in a few hours. **True/False**

7 Driving while high on pot is not as dangerous as driving drunk.
True/False

8 Smoking cigarettes isn't so bad, and I can quit anytime I want to.
True/False

9 Chewing tobacco isn't dangerous and helps me stay alert, especially while playing sports.
True/False

10 I can't turn down having a beer or taking a hit if I want to be popular.
True/False

Answers on next page.

"Test Yourself" Answers

① **False**. Doing coke is like playing Russian roulette. Using it once can kill you, because cocaine can cause your heart to stop beating. It's almost impossible to predict who will be extremely sensitive to cocaine, but teens are more likely to have severe reactions than adults. You never know if "just one time" will be your last time.

② **False.** While partying on the weekends may seem fun and even harmless, the routine can become a habit. Many teens who start out partying only on weekends become addicted to alcohol and other drugs. While they may not drink or do other drugs every day, they can't wait for Friday night to get high. It's almost all they think about.

③ **False.** Although your first drink or two may cause you to loosen up and laugh a lot, alcohol really is a depressant. It slows down your body functions and causes confusion, decreased alertness, poor coordination, blurred vision and drowsiness. Too much alcohol, taken quickly, can even cause death.

④ **True.** Using anabolic steroids can cause many unpleasant side effects, including severe acne, premature baldness, bloating, growth of body hair for females and breast enlargement for males. Plus, regular steroid use can cause more dangerous problems that may not show up for a while, such as high cholesterol, liver and kidney damage, skin tumors and cancer. And many times, users become addicted. Some steroid users also experience "roid rages," which cause them to become violent and unpredictable.

⑤ **True.** Smoking while pregnant is almost like giving your unborn child a cigarette, too. The chemicals in tobacco smoke increase the baby's heart rate, reduce the oxygen supply and slow cell growth. Women who smoke while pregnant have higher rates of premature births, miscarriages and stillbirths than women who do not smoke while pregnant.

6 **False.** The feeling of being high from marijuana may last only a few hours, but your ability to think straight and perform difficult tasks may be adversely affected for as long as 24 hours after you take your last hit.

7 **False.** Driving while under the influence of any drug is extremely dangerous. All drugs, including pot, have a negative effect on your reaction time, coordination and perception. This makes your risk of having a crash extremely high. Even worse, kids who drive high or drunk may think they're driving safely because alcohol and other drugs have a negative effect on the part of the brain responsible for judgment.

8 **False.** Smoking cigarettes is bad news all around. Cigarette smoking can cause lung, throat and mouth cancer, an increased risk of heart attack and chronic breathing problems (bronchitis, emphysema). Besides, it smells and tastes bad, too. And if you think you can quit anytime, think again. Studies have shown that nicotine is among the most difficult addictions to break.

9 **False.** Chewing tobacco carries many of the same risks as cigarette smoking, including addiction and the risk of developing cancer, especially of the mouth, nose and throat.

10 **False.** Although you may want to be part of the crowd, you shouldn't do anything you don't want to do. If you turn down alcohol or other drugs and lose friends as a result, those people probably weren't true friends anyway. Learn the tricks for saying no and having a good time without tobacco, alcohol and other drugs.

—*Kate Delhagen*, STRAIGHT TALK

Chapter 7

CHOOSE YOUR POISON

On a farm in rural South Georgia, a tall, nice-looking boy in his late teens wandered aimlessly around the yard. When you looked into his eyes, you saw a vacant stare. Mentally retarded? No—at least he wasn't born that way.

"He was all right until he started fooling with drugs," his father explained. "He was an honor student in high school and a good athlete. He and some boys got started with drugs—'pot' they call it. Now his mind is affected. He doesn't do anything now but drift around the yard."

Choose your Poison...

"Pot" or "grass" is the thing today. Lots of young people are experimenting with it. Marijuana is considered by many people to be relatively harmless, but it has in it a substance known as THC. This substance can produce delusions and hallucinations. And it can definitely affect the mind. Worst of all, it nearly always introduces a person to more powerful drugs.

David Wilkerson, the author of *THE CROSS AND*

67

THE SWITCHBLADE, is an authority on what happens to drug-users. He has worked with thousands of young people hooked on drugs. He says,

I consider marijuana the most dangerous drug used today.

Marijuana looks innocent and goes by very innocent names like "tea" or "Mary Jane." But "Mary Jane" is no innocent little lady. She's a sneaky doll who has started thousands of unsuspecting young people on the route to mainlining heroin.

I know what marijuana does. It breaks down resistance to other drugs. It paves the way to alcoholism and drug addiction. It destroys moral values, especially sex standards.

There is no question in my mind that anyone who will try marijuana will try LSD. When a kid comes to me and says he is smoking marijuana but that he doesn't intend to go on to other drugs, I know he's not telling the truth. He's started on marijuana because he is not satisfied with life, and he will go the whole route.

Frequently parents will bring a marijuana-smoking son or daughter to me for help, and I can't help them because the smoker has gotten the idea, "I'm not really hooked, and I'll never become a junkie. Tea isn't bad."

I have not been able to help one such smoker. The irony of it is that a year later, the same youngster will come back, dirty and unshaved and hooked on heroin. That's the end of the route.

The first stick of pot you smoke is a symptom of a disease that will destroy you unless you destroy it. Don't take any chances.

Today's marijuana is more potent and more expensive than the pot of a few years back because the amount of THC—the ingredient that causes the high— has risen from 2% or 3% to 12%.

LETHAL, SUICIDAL AND DISASTROUS

LSD is a chemical compound without color or taste, but it is so powerful that an amount the size of an aspirin tablet will affect the minds of 1500 people. No wonder it is called "Lethal, Suicidal and Disastrous."

In California, a sixteen-year-old boy was rushed to the hospital after a bad trip with LSD. There he slashed his wrists with a knife. His life was saved by hospital attendants who got to him just in time. The boy was then left in a room in which everything had been taken out but his bed. The next time he was left alone, he gouged out his eyes with his fingers. Finally, he was found dead. He had killed himself by holding his breath.

LSD use by high school seniors reached its highest levels last year. In the rave clubs of Los Angeles, $2 to $5 buys a teenager a 10 to 12 hour LSD high. Among the effects of putting this poison into your body are bad trips, flashbacks, schizophrenia and brain damage. [1]

Taking any drug or pill without knowing what it is and what it will do is foolish and dangerous. You can permanently damage your mind, your body, and even your unborn child with a chemical you may not even know is there. A young mother who had taken LSD only once had a baby born with a deformed skull and a serious intestinal defect.

COCAINE IS DEADLY

Cocaine or "coke" is made from the leaves of the cocoa bush. It is powerfully addictive. People snort it, smoke it or they can inject it.

Cocaine stimulates the central nervous system and makes users hyper. User's hearts beat very fast when

69

they do cocaine. At the same time the drug causes the blood vessels to contract and narrow while they are trying to handle the additional flow of blood from the heart. Body temperature and blood pressure shoot up and this can cause a stroke, a heart attack or seizure.

In powder form, cocaine can be "snorted." In liquid form, it can be injected into your veins. "Freebase" is a concentrated, solid form of cocaine that can be smoked. Small shavings or lumps of freebase are known as "crack." Smoking crack or freebase cocaine is extremely dangerous. The drug is more potent in this form and it reaches the brain in seconds, giving an intense high.

Coming down from a high on cocaine in any form often triggers an intense craving for more of the drug. This is why it is so addictive. It also explains why some people overdose on it.

Cocaine in any form is deadly. College basketball star Len Bias had a promising future with the pros, but one overdose on cocaine ended his career and his life. It was his first experiment with cocaine . . . and his last.

HEROIN MAKES YOU ITS SLAVE

Many drug abusers, scared off by the devastation of crack, turn to heroin, but this is like jumping from the frying pan into the fire.

The fear of AIDS has caused most heroin users to change from needle injection to snorting. Even so, the risks remain high.

Heroin is a white, odorless, crystalline powder of opium which is found in the poppy plant. It is often "cut" with milk sugar, quinine, baking soda, or even talcum powder.

Once hooked on heroin, the body and mind require heroin every day just to feel normal. If the body does not have its craving fulfilled, withdrawal sickness begins. Those who are trying to quit the habit find that the withdrawal effects are so hellish that many give up the effort and desperately run for another fix.

The high cost of heroin causes the addict to do anything to get more white grains. Girls who become addicts invariably turn to prostitution to get money. One junkie said, "Addiction to heroin is the closest thing to hell itself."

WHY DO TEENS DO DRUGS?

Most teenagers know that drug use is harmful to their bodies and can even kill them. Why, then, do they do it?

Mostly it's peer pressure. They find themselves at a party where marijuana and cocaine are being distributed. Seemingly "everybody is doing it." To refuse makes them "party poopers." Many teens would rather risk their lives than incur the disapproval of their peers.

In a Texas city, some guys decided to play Russian roulette. The first boy tried once, fired, and luckily the chamber was empty.

"Try it again," urged his pals.

And, so, after a few moments he did. Again, a stroke of luck.

"Man, you're really cool," said his friends. "Come on, do it again!"

This time the young man shakily refused to risk his life again.

The name-calling began. "You're chicken . . . yellow . . . you're just chicken!"

The pressure was too much for him. He gave in to his "friends." But this time his luck ran out. The bullet was in the chamber. He died instantly. [2]

When you do drugs to gain the approval of your friends you are risking your life to gain their acceptance.

Maybe you should ask yourself: Is it worth that?

71

WHO'S LEADING THIS CROWD?

Some years ago, a team of scientists were investigating the "schooling" instinct in fish. Large schools of fish swim along together, darting first this way and that. Somehow they seem to move in unison.

By a bit of skillful surgery, these scientists removed a portion of the brain of one fish. After recovery, the fish was placed back in the tank with his original school. Soon the whole school began to follow this strange-acting fish with only part of a brain.

Before you follow a crowd, ask yourself, "Who's leading this crowd?" It might be somebody with only part of a brain! ○ ○ ○ ○ ○ ○

—David Augsburger, *So What? Everybody's Doing It!* © 1969

Chapter 8

"IT'S A BUMMER!"

it's a BUMMER

It's a typical Friday evening for Alcoholics Anonymous in a New Jersey suburb. Everybody is lounging around doing what they must do to stay sober—telling and retelling their dismal tragedies and listening to others.

You have to listen closely to hear what the slight brunette girl is saying. Curled up on the sofa, speaking softly between draws on one cigarette after another, she tells her story:

"I started drinking wine on weekends and right away I just loved getting drunk. Before long my whole life was revolving around getting drunk and stoned, until that's all I was doing. Sometimes I drank a fifth or a quart of whiskey a day, plus smoking pot and taking pills. I was hardly eating. I couldn't stand it any more.

"It got so bad, I didn't feel secure if a bottle wasn't sitting in front of me. Like this was at 11 or 12 years old."

The girl talking is a high school freshman who looks a lot older than her 15 years.

Now a ninth grade boy tells his story:

"My friend's parents were heavy drinkers, with liquor cabinets full of half gallons. We'd take a milk jug, fill it up with liquor and orange juice, and then cruise up to the sand traps on the golf course, or just hang out in some kid's rec room.

"By now all the money I could lay my hands on went for beer and drugs. My mother would give me money to buy something. I'd steal whatever it was I was supposed to buy and then use the money to get drunk or stoned.

"I didn't realize how much we were drinking. My friend and I thought all we had to do was taper off whenever we wanted to.

"A year ago, I was a walking zombie—scared to say hello to anybody, scared to raise my hand in class. That's when I joined A.A."

Everybody here except the host and hostess is in their late teens or early 20's. They all began drinking while they were still in elementary or junior high and were "human garbage cans" by high school, their bodies wasted by booze and dope and their minds fogged.

THE MOST DEVASTATING DRUG OF ALL

Knowing how dangerous drugs are, many young people say, "Man, you've got to be crazy to do drugs. I just stick to my beer and wine." Well, in case you don't know it, the experts say that booze is the worst drug of all.

"The switch is on among young people," says Dr. Morris Chafetz, former director of the National Institute on Alcohol Abuse and Alcohol, "from a wide range of other drugs to the most devastating drug of all—alcohol."

Why does Dr. Chafetz call alcohol "the most devastating drug of all"? Probably because so many people use it, who don't think of it as a drug and don't believe it is dangerous. "The plain and simple fact is," says Dr. Chafetz, "that every time we are drunk, we have overdosed with a drug."

More and more young people are using some form of alcohol and are dependent on it. Many drink heavily and often get drunk. They don't take their dependence on alcohol seriously because they think of it as "Mickey Mouse" compared to other drugs.

76

But alcohol is no "Mickey Mouse." In its various forms it is destroying the lives of more people in America than any other drug.

Julie, 16, tells how she wound up in a rehabilitation center for teenagers: "I started drinking in the seventh grade—ripping off my mom. In the ninth grade, I overdosed on Valium. I tried to kill myself. I was in a psychiatric ward for three months—ran away seven times. A year later I was in detoxification at another hospital."

Why do teenagers drink? Lots of reasons—sociability, going with the crowd, to bring down feelings of anxiety, to enjoy a temporary high.

Most young people (and adults too) have the idea that a can of beer is less intoxicating than a drink of liquor. The fact is that a 12-ounce can of beer, a one-ounce drink of 100-proof liquor, and a six-ounce glass of wine are *equal in their effect on the body.*

Whether it's beer, wine, whiskey, or vodka, the substance that affects you is ethyl alcohol. It's not what you drink, it's how much alcohol goes down your throat. Ethyl alcohol is extremely soluble in water—so soluble in fact, that when you sip it, part of it is absorbed right through your tongue and gums before you have time to swallow it!

When ethyl alcohol gets in your blood stream, it is quickly carried to every organ in your body—especially to your brain. The evidence is that even the moderate drinker may suffer the loss of some irreplaceable brain cells every time he drinks. So if you want to hang on to all of your brain cells, don't drink.

Alcohol is metabolized in the liver. The entire blood supply circulates through the liver every four minutes. Enzymes in the liver change alcohol into acetaldehyde, a highly poisonous chemical. This is then converted into acetate, and finally into carbon dioxide and water.

The process is slow. It takes about three hours for

each ounce of pure alcohol. Virtually nothing will speed up this process in the liver or sober up an intoxicated person. Coffee only produces a wide-awake drunk.

Alcohol washes the vitamins out of your body and makes you more likely to get sick or feel run down. Alcohol adds nothing to your body except fat. Beer especially will give you a lot of unwanted pounds. Everyone is familiar with the "beer belly."

ALCOHOL AND PREGNANCY DON'T MIX

A pregnant woman takes a drink. Within minutes her unborn baby has the same drink. Alcohol damages the vulnerable developing brain. The result—a skinny and retarded baby. It's called Fetal Alcohol Syndrome(FAS).

"You don't have to be an alcoholic to hurt your baby; you just have to be drinking enough and pregnant," says Ann Streissguth, a member of a team that first defined this syndrome. "A really dangerous time is before you know you are pregnant, so the best recommendation is not to drink when planning a pregnancy." [1]

"I THOUGHT MY HEART WOULD BREAK"

"When Malcom was born, I thought my heart would break," said Ellen O'Donovan. Ellen was drinking regularly when she discovered she was pregnant. Months later her son was born with fetal alcohol syndrome.

Malcom was undersized at birth, with kidneys and a stomach that didn't work properly. He had to be tube fed until he was 14 months old. His head is smaller than normal. His face is deformed and he was born with defective vision in both eyes. Surgery later gave him limited vision in one eye.

Ellen has dedicated the rest of her life to taking care of Malcom. She hasn't taken a drink in three and a half years. "Just tell the women out there if they want to have a baby, leave the drink out of it." [2]

78

"DO I HAVE TO DRINK AND PUT OUT TO BE POPULAR?"

Young people often go along with things they themselves do not want to do. Why? Because they think this is the way to win the friendship and respect of others. But it doesn't work that way.

Young people admire a person with courage. They respect a person who has his own beliefs and stands up for them, even if it means standing alone. Here's what one girl says about this:

I am a 16-year-old sophomore. I am a varsity cheerleader and belong to plenty of clubs. I am also considered part of the popular crowd. I do not drink and I am not sexually active, and my friends respect me for that! I have a good attitude about everything and get along with almost everybody.

I have never liked alcohol. Two of my very close friends were injured very badly in drinking accidents. Tom was the first one. He hit head-on with a van. He is now blind and has been in the hospital for eight months. Ann is a senior, a

79

cheerleader and the most popular girl in the school. She hit a tree head-on and has been in a coma for five months. The worst part is that nobody has quit drinking. . . .

About having sex before marriage, I just don't believe that sex is something to abuse. It is supposed to be special and if you do it all the time, then it's not special when you get married. The boys I go out with respect me and do not try to force me to do anything I do not want to do. If they ask me out again, then I know they care, and if they don't, they are not even worth worrying about.

As for being popular or cool, that can be done without drugs, alcohol or sex, and I am living proof of that! —Angela

*Names changed to protect identity.

○ ○ ○ ○ ○ ○

Chapter 9

THE PARTY'S OVER

The Party's Over

It's Saturday night and you're out cruising and boozing with your friends. After a few beers, all you're thinking about is having a good time.

For now, you might think about a few other things. For starters, think about what you will look like when the car you're riding in suddenly looks like a piece of crumpled aluminum foil.

Here's something else you might think about **before** Saturday night: *Drinking and driving, or riding in a car with a driver who has been drinking, is the number one killer of 15 to 24-year-olds.*

Mark Cellon, 16, is not certain about a lot of things, but he is sure about two things.

First, he is sure that neither he nor the other six teenagers who were involved in a head-on crash, in which three teens died, will ever drink and drive.

Second, he is equally certain that the accident will not change the lifestyle of teenagers who did not know those involved in the fatal accident.

"Most teenagers out there think they're invincible," Mark says. "Nothing can happen to them. It takes something like this to make you change."

He was in the back seat of a Mazda compact when it collided head-on with a GMC van at two o'clock in the morning. The accident occurred minutes after the seven teenagers left a party. Travis, the 16-year-old driver, and two 17-year-old girls in the front seat were killed instantly. Mark and three others in the back seat and the two people in the van survived with severe injuries.

Mark said that drinking was not excessive at the party. He said he had three or four beers. "Before we left, Travis was juggling bowling pins, his speech wasn't slurred and he was walking straight." But Travis was later found to have a blood alcohol level of 0.15 percent, which made him a drunken driver under state law.

Mark expects to speak against drunk driving at local high schools, though he is not sure it will do any good. "Then another side of me says, 'Just maybe, what if one person listens and that person doesn't do it.' To save one life, that would be worth it."

If you're caught with alcohol or other drugs in your car, or if you're pulled over for driving under the influence of alcohol or any illegal substance, you will be faced with a number of unpleasant things.

Like being back in your walking shoes for quite a while. Like a fine and jail time. Like court costs and legal fees of at least $500. Like having your car insurance triple for at least three years. Like making it difficult for your parents to trust you.

What are the best ways of avoiding a DUI charge? *Don't drink.* If you know that alcohol will be served at a party, bring your own non-alcoholic drink. Or just stay away from parties where alcohol and drugs will be used.

Don't get into a car with a friend who has been drinking. Tell your date or friend that someone else is driving you home. Call a parent or a friend or a relative to come get you, or take a cab.

Find some friends who don't use illegal substances. Joe couldn't understand why he shouldn't run around with the drinking crowd. After all, he didn't drink. No, but his drinking friend DID . . . and it was his drinking friend who was driving the car in which Joe was killed.

○○○○○ ○

What Did He Lose?

A teenager is stopped for a traffic violation. The cop recognizes a certain odor in his car and discovers that he has a few "joints" with him.

He comes before the court and is convicted of marijuana possession, an automatic felony. The judge gives him a suspended sentence.

Maybe you think that's a pretty light sentence and nothing to worry about, but let's see what it means.

A **felony is a major crime** which is punishable by death or imprisonment in a state prison. A suspended sentence means that he doesn't have to go to prison unless he gets in trouble again.

Being a convicted felon is heavy stuff. This guy can never get it off his record. It marks him for life. And he lost some very important rights.

WHAT DID HE LOSE?

- **He lost his right** to vote.
- **He lost his right** to own a gun.
- **He lost the right** to run for public office.
- **He cannot** be admitted to West Point, Annapolis or the Air Force Academy.
- **He lost the chance** to ever be a licensed doctor, dentist, certified public accountant, engineer, lawyer, architect, realtor, school teacher, barber, funeral director or stockbroker.
- **He can never get a job where** he has to be bonded or licensed.
- **He can't work for** the city, county, state or federal government.

All of this is what he lost.

○ ○ ○ ○ ○   ○

Chapter 10

THE DEADLY DRAG

○○○○○　○

the DEADly Drag...

A jumbo jet with 274 people on board misses the runway, crashes and bursts into flame. There are no survivors. This happens four times in one day!

The newspapers can't find large enough block type to report these disasters. Tom Brokaw, Dan Rather and the other evening news anchors go ballistic. 1,096 people killed in one day in freak accidents.

But wait! The next day, the same thing happens, and the next day, and the next day. The whole nation is in total shock!

This scenario has never happened, and we hope that it never will happen. But there is another scenario that happens every day. *One thousand ninety-six people die from cigarette smoking everyday, 365 days in the year.* That's in this country alone. Like the victims of an airplane crash, they leave behind grieving relatives and friends.

It's no wonder that the cigarette companies have to spend billions of dollars each year on advertising. They have to replace the 1,096 "regular customers" who die from their products every day.

Who fills most of the shoes of the 1,096 people who die each day from cigarette smoking? *Teenagers.*

Every year a million teenagers take up smoking. In fact, 90 percent of all smokers started as teenagers. Most start between the eighth and tenth grades. Most all of them expect to be able to stop anytime they want to and certainly before becoming adults. But it doesn't work that way.

Nicotine is a powerfully addictive drug. It will hook you faster than alcohol or other drugs. And, for most people, it's harder to quit smoking than it is to quit drinking or doing drugs.

BECOMING A NICOTINE ADDICT

You should know the three simple stages to becoming a nicotine addict. First, you try out cigarettes. They taste terrible, but maybe you gain acceptance with the smoking crowd.

The second stage is smoking occasionally—like at parties or on dates. When others light up, you do too.

The third stage is when you cross the line between being an occasional smoker to a hard-core smoker. You're hooked! This usually comes as a surprise. Most teens are hooked by the time they are sixteen.

WHAT HAPPENS WHEN YOU LIGHT UP?

When you take a puff, carbon monoxide (that same black smoke that comes out of your car exhaust pipe—*yucko!*) enters your blood, and cancer-causing agents enter your lungs. Among the poisons you are inhaling are arsenic, cyanide, formaldehyde, ammonia, tar, carbon dioxide and nicotine.

Each cigarette contains about 4,000 different chemicals. Forty of these are known to be cancer-causing. (Some are the same ingredients used in rat poisons, weed killers, and insecticides—*gross!*)

Tar, the dark, sticky mixture that forms when tobacco burns, contains hundreds of chemicals known to cause cancer. You can see it on your teeth and on your fingers. When it gets into the lungs, it sticks to them. On the autopsy table, it's easy to tell whether a person was a smoker or a non-smoker. The lungs of a non-smoker are pink in color. The lungs of people who smoke are black.

Guys, you can't be much of an athlete if your lungs are coated with that black tar.

DOES SMOKING MAKE A GIRL MORE APPEALING TO GUYS?

Apparently not.

Some guys won't date a girl who smokes. Here's what three guys said about girls who light up:

It's a turn-off. It makes their clothes smell when you're near them. John, 17, Hollywood, CA

I had a girlfriend who smoked and I had to break up with her—her breath smelled so bad! I couldn't kiss her! 17-year-old Greg

I don't think it's sexy, I think it's repulsive. It's not flattering. Chad, Phoenix, AZ

IS SMOKING REALLY THAT BAD FOR YOU?

Smoking makes you smell bad and feel awful. It can spoil your looks because it wipes out the vitamin B in your body, yellows your teeth and stains your hands.

"When the cells in your body come in contact with the cancer-causing ingredients in cigarettes, they grow out of control," says Rodney Geir, M.D., a cancer specialist. "The results are cancers that are horribly painful and disfiguring."

Exposure to tobacco is extremely risky to babies both before and after they are born. Pregnant women who smoke have a greater number of stillbirths and their babies are more likely to die within the first few months. One other thing, women who smoke are three times more likely to become infertile—unable to ever have a baby—than those who do not smoke.

The health risks may not seem very real to you now, but down the road, they will be when you have an early heart attack. Or maybe you're just feeling lousy so you go to your doctor and he discovers that you have lung or throat cancer or emphysema. It may be too late then to do anything about it.

Smoking makes you very unpopular with non-smokers. For good reason, too. Your second-hand smoke is more deadly to others than the smoke you inhale because it actually contains more tar, nicotine and carbon monoxide. Your smoke puts other people at risk of cancer and other killing diseases, and they don't exactly love you for this. Furthermore, the smelly cigarette odor clings to their hair and clothes.

WHAT WILL HAPPEN IF I DECIDE TO QUIT?

It won't be easy breaking the nicotine habit, but millions do it each year and are glad they did.

Within days of quitting, you will feel better. Your sense of taste and smell will sharpen. Food will taste better. You will have more energy. If you have had problems with your complexion, they may clear up. You will gain a lot more confidence knowing that you—not cigarettes—are running your life.

WON'T I GAIN WEIGHT IF I QUIT?

You don't have to gain weight. Avoid high-calorie foods and start exercising. That will not only control your weight, but you will look better and feel better.

WHAT ABOUT SMOKELESS TOBACCO?

Sean Marsee was a track star at his high school in Oklahoma. He was a month away from graduating when he noticed a red spot with a hard white core forming on his tongue. Sean had always taken good care of himself. He was careful about what he ate. He didn't smoke or drink. He lifted weights and ran every day.

But Sean had been chewing and spitting tobacco since he was 12 years old. The white spot on his tongue turned out to be cancer. Doctors carved out a third of his tongue. After several operations to try to stop the cancer, Sean's face was mutilated. A friend who came to see him in the hospital fainted when he saw Sean. The cancer spread quickly throughout his body. Sean died less than a year after graduation.

If you're thinking of using snuff or chewing tobacco, Sean has some advice for you: "Don't use smokeless tobacco, and don't start." That's the message Sean wrote down before he died. [1]

A GOOD USE FOR CIGARETTES

A cigarette company sent a complimentary pack of cigarettes to a high school guy with a note that said, "We hope that you will find these useful."

In a few weeks, he wrote back, "Thank you for sending the cigarettes. I sure did find them useful. I soaked them in water and sprayed this liquid on our vegetables and it killed all the bugs in the garden."

THE MARLBORO MAN IS *dead!*

He was a man's man—the handsome, macho man with his neatly-trimmed mustache, steel-grey eyes, and the rolled-brim western hat. You remember him. He had that patriotic eagle tattooed on his hand. He was strong. He was free. He was the John Wayne type who rode the range, punching cows or rounding up wild horses, like real men did in the Old West.

As he took a drag on his Marlboro, he beckoned us to come to the place of freedom—"Come where the flavor is. Come to Marlboro country." The Marlboro man won't be making any more of those commercials. He's dead. Lung cancer killed him. He was 51.

What many of us did not know is something the cigarette companies will never tell us. The Marlboro man spent the last three years of his life warning young people of the dangers of smoking. He knew that it was too late for him, but he spent those years telling others that what he had portrayed in those commercial and ads was a lie. His message was, "Real freedom and enjoyment is never getting hooked on cigarettes."

The Blythe Banner

WARNING TO A TEENAGE GIRL

—Harry F. Casey

On my way to work this morning I drove past the high school. As usual, I saw hordes of young people on their way to class. My attention was drawn to a particularly attractive girl, about 15.

She puffed on a cigarette as she walked with her friends, laughing, joking, flirting. She was vibrant with life—so like my wife, Shirley.

I called Shirl "Smiley Big Eyes." She had a smile that filled up her face, eyes that lighted up my life.

She was just barely legal when I met her, round in all the right places and consumed with a wholesome zest for being and doing.

Her high-school yearbook from Conway, N.H., said Shirley Francis had been voted "best all-around." She was all girl, but she could throw a baseball like a man. She was a lifeguard swimmer. She could ski down snowy slopes in a reckless, daring way. She could dance all night and still be bright-eyed for work in the morning. She could talk politics, ideas, philosophies. I taught her to ride a horse, and she'd follow me on the roughest trails. We camped, fished and hunted. She could shoot, bait a hook and cook over a campfire.

She bore us four fine children and then learned to water ski—single ski better than I—and drive a boat . . . when she wasn't washing diapers.

Every time she bought groceries she got a carton of cigarettes.

Just like that young girl I watched this morning, Shirl started to smoke when she was 15. It was the in-thing to do. Nobody told her it was bad for her health. In the late 1940s, there were no Surgeon General's warnings. And just as Shirley Francis did everything full tilt, she smoked that way—more than anyone else.

So I watched that healthy body erode to 80 pounds. I saw the premature aging of the heavy smoker. I cared for her through heart disease and an operation to replace an artery. When they found tumors in her neck I went with her to the chemotherapy treatments, held her hand and watched her agony as the chemicals worked on her body. Later I saw the burns from radiation treatments.

Shirl gave it every shot. I was proud of her fight for life. But I'll never forget how the morning cough of 20 years ago gradually changed into that racking, choking strangle. I held her as she struggled in the night to suck air into her lungs—until even my gentle embrace pained her tumor-filled body.

She was just 50 when she died of lung cancer.

I hope that young girl I watched this morning happens to read this. She should have seen my Shirl. She's just like her.   Condensed from *The Rustler*

Sometime's it doesn't pay to follow the crowd...

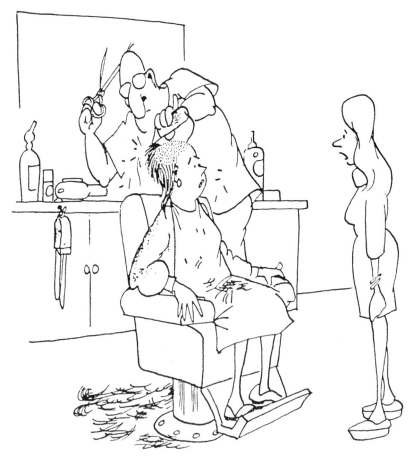

OH, NO! I'M TOO LATE! I JUST TALKED TO TRACY AND IT TURNS OUT IT'S JUST THE BOYS WHO ARE HAVING IT DONE!

—*Bill Maul*

Chapter 12

HOW TO SAY NO
(NICELY)

○○○○○ ○

HOW TO SAY *NO* (NICELY)

Can you say no without feeling like a jerk, and without putting down your friends? Here are a few suggestions:

❶ Decide ahead of time what you will and won't do. If you're headed for a party and you suspect people will be drinking there, settle on an answer **before** you walk in the door and someone shoves a beer into your hand. Or if your friends are going to group up on an assignment that's supposed to be done solo, decide what you are going to say before your friends pass out textbooks and pencils. With this advanced planning you won't be caught off guard. You'll also gain a sense of confidence and control over your choices.

2 **Be friendly yet firm.** You'll find that people respect someone who can be an individual without being a snob. Your friendliness and confidence may convince other less-confident bystanders to say no as well.

3 **Be honest.** Something's awry [*bad wrong*] when you have to lie in order to avoid doing something you don't think is right. Simply state the truth and leave it at that. If you're sick and tired of your group of friends putting down the class nerd, let them know it. If you don't like beer, say so. If you do like it, say, "Looks good, but I think I'll have a Coke instead." If you feel uncomfortable going to an R-rated movie, say so.

4 **Speak for others when they won't speak for themselves.** As we have seen, we can—and should— use peer pressure for good. If your friend is ready to drive drunk, you should do everything you can to get him or her out from behind the wheel. Along with refusing to ride with this person, you should do your best to keep your friend from harming others—including him or herself. Or if your group is constantly putting someone down, you shouldn't just stand aside and let it happen. Let your displeasure be known— tactfully yet firmly.

One way to deal with this is to suggest an alternative. Push for a different movie, ask for a Coke instead of beer, initiate a "cram session" the day before the test for anyone who wants to come, subtly move the conversation away from gossip by asking a question about something else. Remember, others may feel the same way you do and may simply need someone to speak up.

⑤ Speak for yourself. There is an exception to almost every rule, including the one above. What if you have tried to get your group to do what is right, but there is no positive response? Do you keep nagging or hassling? No. In the end, you're not responsible for everyone else's actions—only your own. If the others won't respond after you've made your opinion known, don't just shrug your shoulders and keep carrying on. Refuse to be involved in something you believe is wrong.

⑥ Affirm the person; reject the action. If you're getting pressure from friends, assure them that you want to be with them but not when they're doing what you feel is wrong. Separate the activity from the person.

⑦ Appeal to laws and rules. If someone asks you to break the law or to break the stated rules of your school, home, or job, don't feel guilty about saying no. Simply say that you'd rather stick by the rules.

⑧ Appeal to possible consequences.
"My parents would kill me if they ever found out I went there!"
"I'd rather not risk getting suspended for cheating."
"No thanks. I'm driving tonight and don't want to take any chances."

⑨ Accept the possibility of rejection. Even if you decline graciously and don't condemn your friends, someone may feel resentful and snub you. This may hurt, but if you endure the pain and seek out friends who are more accepting, you'll be better off in the long run.   —Verne Becker, *Peer Pressure*, © 1987 Campus Life Books

○ ○ ○ ○ ○   ○

Chapter 13

THINK RIGHT !
FEEL RIGHT !

○○○○○ ○

think RIGHT !

feel RIGHT !

Our happiness in life depends a great deal on our attitudes. Our attitude toward ourselves is perhaps the most important attitude of all because it has such a profound effect on our life.

This attitude toward ourselves has a special name. It is called "self-image." Our self-image is the way we see ourselves.

Our self-image is important because it affects our attitude toward our family, our friends and others. People who have a poor self-image usually have trouble getting along with other people. Generally they are unhappy.

Those who study and understand human behavior tell us that *we are controlled by the way we inwardly see ourselves.* To put it another way, you are going to act out the way you think about yourself.

Does it really matter what you think about yourself? Yes, it does. If you think you're a piece of junk, you act like you are junk, and you feel like junk.

Here is a strange fact: We are often totally mistaken in the way we see ourselves. A girl may be nice looking and have a good personality, but because she wasn't elected cheerleader, she thinks she is not worth much. A guy may have a lot going for him, but because he is not a star athlete, he has a poor image.

Whether an idea is false or not, if we believe it, we will be controlled by it.

In his book, *Love Yourself,* Walter Trobish relates this incident:

> *The girl entered our hotel room. It was the day after my wife and I had given a lecture at a university in northern Europe. The hotel room was the only place we had for counseling.*
>
> *She was a beautiful Scandinavian girl. Long blond hair fell over her shoulders. Gracefully she sat down in the armchair offered to her and looked at us with deep and vivid blue eyes. Her long arms allowed her to fold her hands over her knees. We noticed her fine, slender fingers, revealing a very tender, precious personality.*
>
> *As we discussed her problems, we came back again and again to one basic issue which seemed to be the root of all the others. It was the problem which we had least expected when she entered the room: She could not love herself. In fact, she hated herself to such a degree*

that she was only one step away from putting an end to her life.

To point out to her the apparent gifts she had— her success as a student, the favorable impression she had made upon us by her outward appearance—seemed to be of no avail. She was afraid that any self-appreciation she might express would mean giving in to the temptation of pride. . . .

We asked her to stand up and take a look in the mirror. She turned her head away. With gentle force I held her head so that she had to look into her own eyes. She cringed as if she were experiencing physical pain.

It took a long time before she was able to whisper, though unconvinced, the sentence I asked her to repeat, "I am a beautiful girl."

YOU ARE PRICELESS!

Every person is a one-of-a-kind, priceless individual. Sometimes it takes another person to convince us of our worth.

A little girl was born with a birth defect which caused her to look different from other children. When she went to school, her classmates hurt her by the unkind things they said. But seven simple words from her second-grade teacher changed this little girl's life forever. Here is her story:

I grew up knowing I was different, and I hated it. I was born with a cleft palate, and when I started school my classmates made it clear to me how I must look to others; a little girl with a misshapen lip, crooked nose, lopsided teeth and garbled speech.

When schoolmates would ask, "What happened to your lip?" I'd tell them I'd fallen and cut it on a piece of glass. Somehow it seemed more accept-

able to have suffered an accident than to have been born different. I was convinced that no one outside my family could love me. Or even like me. Then I entered Mrs. Leonard's second-grade class.

Mrs. Leonard was round and pretty and fragrant, with shining brown hair and warm, dark, smiling eyes. Everyone adored her. But no one came to love her more than I did. And for a special reason.

The time came for the annual hearing tests given at our school. I could barely hear out of one ear and was not about to reveal something else that would single me out as different. So I cheated.

The "whisper test" required each child to go to the classroom door, turn sideways, close one ear with a finger, while the teacher whispered something from her desk, which the child repeated. Then the same for the other ear. Nobody checked how tightly the untested ear was covered, so I merely pretended to block mine.

As usual, I was last. But all through the testing I wondered what Mrs. Leonard might say to me. I knew from previous years that the teacher whispered things like "The sky is blue" or "Do you have new shoes?"

My time came. I turned my bad ear toward her, plugging up the other just enough to be able to hear. I waited, and then came the words . . . seven words that changed my life forever.

Mrs. Leonard, the teacher I adored, said softly, "I wish you were my little girl." [1]

This girl's life was changed because of seven words which her teacher spoke to her. Those words— "I wish you were my little girl "—showed her that her teacher loved and respected her and considered her a precious little girl.

THINK RIGHT! FEEL RIGHT!

Our happiness in life does not depend on how beautiful or how handsome we are. It does not depend on how smart we are. It does not depend on how much money we have. It depends on our attitude and our actions. Right thoughts lead to right actions and right feelings.

Let's look at five things that can help you be the person you want to be.

Step I. Take Stock of Yourself

Take a good look at yourself in a mirror. What do you see? Do you see someone who is neat, attractive and pleasant looking? You don't have to win a beauty prize. A friendly smile makes anyone attractive if his/her clothes are clean and becoming.

While you are taking a good, objective look at yourself, be sure that you consider any faults that you can overcome. Are you inclined to be lazy? Are you inclined to be irritable? Do you gossip? You don't like those qualities in other people, so determine in your mind that you will get rid of any fault that keeps you from being your best.

Step 2. Be Friendly

Lisa said, "I'm the kind of person who looks at building friendships as a kind of challenge." She determined to smile and be friendly no matter how others responded. What happened? Here's her story.

When I started high school as a freshman, I saw a lot of sour faces in the hallway. It seemed like nobody was happy; nobody smiled. Everybody was a stranger and appeared determined to stay that way.

I decided to do something about it: I would smile and say Hi to kids in the hall until others started smiling and saying Hi back. For days it seemed like nobody noticed. If they did, they would simply look away. It was rather depressing.

But each day after school I would go home and say to my mom, "I won't give up until somebody smiles back." In time one kid smiled, another said Hi. And before long, I saw expressions change on some people's faces. Other kids took the initiative and smiled without being smiled at.

I know it's just a little thing, but I'm still friends with some of the kids I met through a Hi and a smile. This is something I think anybody can do to break the ice. [2]

Step 3. Concentrate on Others

Forget yourself and concentrate on others. Don't think always, "What am I getting out of this?" Instead, ask yourself, "What can I give to this friendship?"

Other people are lonely. Everybody needs love, and people have other needs as well. Concentrate on meeting those needs. The way to have a good friend is to be a good friend.

Step 4. Treasure Friends

Treasure the friends you have and look for more. And it's great to have friends other than those of your own age. Make friends with elderly people and make friends with your little sister's chums.

Here is a special key for people who find it difficult to talk with others. We like people who like us and make us feel important. Remember this when you meet new friends. Encourage them to talk about themselves. Ask their opinion. Listen to their answers. Remember what they tell you so you can refer to it next time you are together.

Step 5. Be Yourself

You don't have to be like somebody else. Every person

is a one-of-a-kind individual. Just be yourself. You don't have to do what others are doing.

You've already met my friend, Shep. He told us why he chose to say no to sex before marriage. I wish you could meet this guy personally. He's tall and really nice looking, but he's rather shy and very modest. Just meeting him, you would have no idea of his accomplishments.

Among other things Shep was the most popular guy in a high school of 1400. He's quick to tell you that he wasn't the best athlete in the school nor the most handsome guy.

Shep didn't go along with the crowd, doing things that were against his beliefs, just to get the other kids to like him. So how did he do it? Here's his story:

"MY POPULARITY RESTED ON TWO THINGS . . ."

The high school I attended had about 1400 students. I was friends with most of them, and was involved in all kinds of sports and activities. I was a captain of the football team, I was a two-year letterman in wrestling, and in my senior year I took up track and field, where I "lettered" in throwing the discus. I was voted "Mr. Northwest High School" in my senior year.

I say these things not to blow my own horn, but to establish that I was not a nerd. You see, when I tell people that I am a virgin, I'm afraid they might automatically file me into some category of nerds, geeks, or fanatics.

Now, I don't claim to be anything special. My popularity in high school rested on two things. I was confident, and I was friendly. I was not overly attractive or overly wealthy. I was just comfortable with myself, and I think that is why people felt comfortable around me. I think that most everyone knew that I studied hard, that I didn't drink or have sex or other things like that, but I never tried to impose my views on them.

What I did do was really try to be everyone's friend, and mostly I was. Maybe that is why I never really felt the peer pressure that I always heard about on television. Every now and then someone would try to give me a hard time, but I would just joke around with them and not let it get to me.

I had my beliefs and I wasn't ashamed of them, but I didn't flaunt them either. Sex was undoubtedly my biggest temptation.

Since I knew, however, that I really did not want to have sex before I got married, I went out with girls who I knew wouldn't be looking to get that from me right off the bat. I had some close calls, but somehow managed to refrain. At the time, I thought I was going to explode, but now I am happy and I know that I made the right decision.

Shep

Chapter 14

HOW TO BE A WINNER!

○○○○○ ○

HOW TO
BE A *Winner!*

Have you ever looked at a winner and thought, "Man, I'd like to be like that! But I don't have much of a chance."?

Are winners some kind of super people who never fail? No, not really. Everybody fails at some time or other. Just because you have failed at something doesn't make you a failure for life.

The important thing is what you do with your failures. Some people complain. Some feel sorry for themselves and hold a pity-party. Some blame others. Some get discouraged. Some quit. Some get up and go at it again.

We're going to consider four real-life people. As you read the brief facts concerning each man, decide in your mind how you would classify him—whether you would consider him a winner or a loser.

Example #1 Winner Loser

This man was born into a very poor family. When he grew up, he tried business but failed. He then decided to go into politics. He ran for a political office and was defeated. He ran again and again, but was defeated. In fact, out of eleven tries, he was defeated nine times.

Example #2 Winner Loser

This man was a major league baseball player. He held the world's record for strikeouts! He fanned out 1,339 times. One thousand, three hundred, thirty-nine times, he came to bat, fanned out, and took that long, humiliating walk from home plate to the dug-out.

Example #3 Winner Loser

As a young man, he wanted to be a military leader or a great statesman, but things didn't go well for him. Three times he took the exams to enter the British Military Academy, and three times he failed.

Example #4 Winner Loser

This man was a scientist. He liked to invent things, but it wasn't easy. He conducted thousands of experiments that failed. For years he worked on a certain invention that he felt would be of great value to the world, but he kept failing. One time he worked day and night on it for three weeks, and then it was only partially successful.

Did you mark these men as "Winners" or "Losers"? Most likely you checked them as "Losers." Certainly all of them failed many times.

Now let's see who these men were and what they did.

Example #1 was Abraham Lincoln—the man who became the sixteenth president of the United States. He is considered one of the greatest presidents this country ever had.

Example #2 was the immortal Babe Ruth, probably the most famous baseball player who ever lived. Until recently he held the world's record for home runs, and that's what people remember about Babe Ruth. "Isn't it strange?" Babe Ruth once said, "I'm the home-run king, but nobody ever asks me how many times I've struck out."

When a reporter asked Babe Ruth, "What is the secret of your success?" he answered, "It's the same as the secret of success anywhere else in life. You have to keep coming up to bat, and keep swinging."

Example #3 was none other than Winston Churchill, England's Prime Minister during World War II. He is regarded by many historians as the greatest statesman of the twentieth century.

Churchill was noted for his bulldog tenacity. Whatever he attempted to do, he went at it with full determination and kept at it until he succeeded.

On one occasion Winston Churchill was scheduled to speak at a graduation ceremony. Everyone waited to hear what this great leader would say. When he got up, Churchill spoke only seven words. In his deep, booming voice, slowly and with determination, Winston Churchill said, "Never . . . never . . . never . . . never . . . never . . . give up!"

Example #4 was Thomas A. **Edison**, the most prolific inventor who ever lived. His inventions include the light bulb, the phonograph, the movie camera, the microphone, the stock ticker. All told, he patented 1,093 inventions—a record that has never been topped by any individual.

He worked long and hard to perfect the light bulb. It is said that he had over 1,500 failures before he succeeded with this invention. He kept trying different things for the filament, but the filament kept breaking. Then, one night, he used a piece of carbonized sewing thread. Forty hours later the bulb was still burning. Edison said to his staff, "If it will burn that number of hours now, I know I can make it burn a hundred." And he did.

When someone asked him if he regretted the time and effort he had spent on the 1,500 failures, he replied, "No, not at all. I learned 1,500 ways that it could **not** be done."

What was the secret of Edison's success? Undoubtedly he was a brilliant man, *but the great factor in his success was his **incredible persistence**.* Nearly all of his inventions came after thousands of experiments that failed. But he learned from his failures and kept trying. It was Edison who said, "Genius is one percent inspiration and 99 percent perspiration."

FAILING AT SOMETHING DOESN'T MAKE YOU A FAILURE

These four examples hammer home one thing: **Just because you fail at something doesn't mean that you are a failure.** There is a ton of difference between failing and being a failure.

Each of these men failed time and time again, but they didn't quit. They could have said, "I'm just a failure. I'll never succeed. I'm going to give up." But they didn't do that. They hung in there and succeeded.

Now let's look at three keys to success: Desire, Determination, and Discipline.

DESIRE

Desire means that you want to do something. You want to be something. Nobody gets anywhere without desire.

All the opportunities in the world won't do you any good unless you want to accomplish something with your life. If you shoot at nothing, you are sure to hit it every time.

Do you have a goal in life? Nobody gets anywhere without a goal. Don't be afraid to dream big dreams. Almost any right dream can be realized.

DETERMINATION

Desire alone won't get the job done. *Your desire must be backed up by determination.*

Some people never try anything for fear of failing. Learn to say, "I'll try," instead of "I can't." It's surprising what a person can do when he determines to do it.

The year was 1916. A seven-year-old boy and his brother were building a fire in the little pot-bellied stove that warmed the one-room schoolhouse.

They put in the paper and then the kindling wood. Then, to get the fire going, they dashed on what they thought was kerosene.

A devastating explosion took place. Somehow, in the meeting the night before, gasoline had been substituted for the kerosene. The two boys were hurled outside as flaming torches.

One brother was killed instantly. The other was terribly burned—especially his legs. The doctor said he had done all he could, but he did not believe the boy would ever walk again. Indeed, he was hoping that he would not have to amputate his legs.

But this boy was determined, and he told the doctor that he would walk again. Yes, he insisted that he would even run again!

Weeks passed into months. The family was encouraged by the boy's determination. Daily his legs were massaged, and gradually feeling returned to the muscles.

Time passed. The doctor and the neighbors were amazed to see this 12-year-old boy running almost everywhere. It was a kind of hippity-hop, but he was running. One leg was still not functioning right, but he was getting more speed all the time.

In grammar school one day he noticed a display of medals in the trophy showcase. He determined to enter the games the next time they were played. He

did. To everyone's amazement, he won first place in the running event.

In high school he continued to run and to win. He planned to go on to college and began to save money for this. But a financial disaster wiped out his savings. He determined to go on anyway. He attended classes in the morning and worked at night to pay his way.

He continued to run, and run, and run. Before long he was setting new track records at Dartmouth College.

In 1938, he set a new record for the indoor mile. The boy whom the doctor had said would never walk had become the fastest miler in the entire United States. His name—Glenn Cunningham.

DISCIPLINE

Discipline means doing what you should do, whether you feel like it or not.

Many people have the idea that success in life depends on whether or not "you've got it." They think, "Either you've got it or you haven't. If you've got it, you're sure to be a success. And if you haven't got it, you're sure to be a failure."

Nothing is farther from the truth. Some people do have more natural ability than others, but that doesn't guarantee success. The world is full of brilliant, talented people who never amount to much because they don't discipline themselves.

Ability can be developed. Ask any coach. He sees it happen all the time—some player with all the natural ability in the world fizzles out while others with less ability make it by desire, determination, and discipline.

Jim Ryan was an Olympic champion runner. It is no accident that he was a champion. In preparation for the Olympics, he ran 150 miles a week *for years.*

"NEVER . . .

NEVER . . .

NEVER . . .

NEVER . . .

NEVER

GIVE UP!"

Winston Churchill

To be successful in any field takes hours upon hours of practice over a long period of time. You don't just luck into being a great musician, a great athlete, or a great anything else. Feeling sorry for yourself and complaining won't change things, but discipline and hard work will.

Ernest Hemingway was one of America's most famous writers. In addition to many other honors, he won the Nobel Prize in 1954 for his book, *Farewell to Arms*.

After writing for so many years, you would think that it came easy for him. But it didn't. Would you like to guess how many times he re-wrote the last chapter of *Farewell to Arms*? Five times? Ten times? Twenty times?

Actually, he re-wrote the last chapter 39 times. That's right—**thirty-nine times.**

Maybe you are one of those who wait until the last minute to get started on a job. You have to hand in a theme paper on Friday, so what do you do? You fool around until Thursday night, and after a few phone calls and a little TV watching, you turn to the task of writing your theme. You write it out, make a few changes, and decide that you are too sleepy to work anymore on it.

You intend to get up in the morning and go over it, but you get up late and have to rush to make it to school. You hand in your paper, hoping for the best. When it comes back, you complain, "I really worked hard on that paper and the teacher gave me a 'C'."

When that happens, instead of complaining about what the teacher gave you, think about Ernest Hemingway and the 39 times he re-wrote the last chapter of his book. Try rewriting your paper five times, or even three and see if it doesn't make a difference in your grade.

"HOW HARD SHOULD I TRY?"

You ask, "How hard should I try? How many times should I try before I give up?" That's something you have to decide for yourself. But remember what Babe Ruth said about success—*"You have to keep coming up to bat and keep swinging."* You never know—the next try may bring success.

"You have to keep coming up to bat and keep swinging!"
Babe Ruth

*The fear you feel when
you love someone and
say "no" to him . . .
may seem awesome
and devastating to you
now—but the greater
pain comes when you
say "yes" and he tires
of you, calling you
"not the kind of girl
he wants to marry."*

Chapter 14

JUST FOR GIRLS

WHAT IS IT LIKE TO BE A GIRL?

"It is a mixture of contradictions...no longer a child...nor yet a woman...your identity is still forming...you are still searching to discover the full reality of who you are...and so everything about your life is in a flux.

"Nothing is the same for you. Not your body. Not your emotions. Not other people's expectations of you. Not other people's responses to you. Not your future. Everything is changing, and change is always frightening.'"[1]

Things are changing, but don't rush the growing-up process. Once you get to be an adult, that's what you're going to be from then on, so why rush things? Those who rush things end up bored with life by the time they're seventeen. For them, there's nothing exciting left to do but get married. And even that won't be too exciting

because they've already
done it all.

Sure, you're interested
in guys. What girl isn't?
But build caring friendships.
Friends don't break up. Lovers
do. Remember, you will
eventually break up with
everyone you date or fall in
love with—except for the one
you marry. If you develop
a deep intimacy with your
dating partners, you will end
up with cheap sex instead
of precious love.

In her book, **Passion And Purity**, noted author Elisabeth Elliot tells of the experiences she went through as a girl and as a young lady, madly in love with a handsome young man. She said that, when she was a young girl, her mother gave her two rules concerning boys and dating:

Rule #1: Don't chase boys!

Rule #2: Keep them at arm's length.

She said, "My mother could have left off the second one. I couldn't get one *within* arm's length! I was a wall flower (wasn't asked out) in high school and college."

In her teen years, Elisabeth made a rule for herself which seemed crazy to all her friends, but it worked. She said, "I decided that I wouldn't even hold hands with a boy, let alone kiss one...Nobody was going to put *me* on any 'bargain table.'"

In college, she had little money so she had to live frugally. She said, "I had two skirts, three sweaters, and a few blouses, which I did my best to mix and match so that it looked as though I was wearing different outfits...My hair gave me an awful time. It was blond, hadn't a hint of bend in it, and grew about an inch a month. I could only afford one permanent a year. In between times, I relied on the old pin-curl system, twirling strands of hair around my finger every night before I went to bed, securing them with a bobby pin.

"If I couldn't do much with my hair, I could do less with my face. Like most girls, I wished I were pretty, but it seemed futile to tamper much with what I had been given, beyond using a cautious touch of pale lipstick (something called Tangee which cost ten cents) and a pat of powder on my nose."

In college she became deeply interested in a handsome young man named Jim Elliot, but she dared not indicate to him her interest. In fact, she didn't allow herself to think about it much because it seemed impossible. She said, "He was a B.M.O.C.—Big Man on Campus—and I was nobody. He was a B.T.O.—Big Time Operator—and I was a T.W.O.—a Teenie Weenie Operator."

Nevertheless, in her senior year, Jim asked her to go for a walk one day. In broad daylight, to her amazement, he confessed his love for her. Five years later, they were married.

In her book Elisabeth Elliot gives some good advice for girls:

- The girl holds the key. A fellow is going to be just about as much a gentleman as what she expects of him and holds him to.
- What attracts men in women is femininity, affirmation, encouragement and tenderness.
- Keep your distance. Recognize that fundamental anomaly of human nature, that we prize what we cannot easily get. We take for granted and even come to despise that which costs us no effort.
- Don't allow a boy to kiss you if he is not serious. Until you find out that this is the right one, don't do anything. Draw the line ahead of time. Don't wait until you are in the back seat...You don't lose anything by restraining your emotions.[2]

If you are a virgin, treasure your virginity. Keep yourself for the one you will want to spend your life with someday. There is no greater gift that you can bring to your husband on your wedding night than your virginity.

CAUTION: When you meet the one you think is Mr.

Right, do *not* lower your standards. Planning to marry is not marriage. Even being engaged is not the same as being married. Engagements are frequently broken. Wait until you are married—until the knot is tied!

Many girls have set their standards and held them until they met, or thought they had met, Mr. Right. Somehow it seemed all right to go all the way with this person. Many who made this mistake have said, "I kept my standards until I met the one I thought I would marry." All regretted the mistake of lowering their standards.

Even if you do marry Mr. Right, you will regret having had sex before your wedding day. You will have destroyed the beauty of that first night together as husband and wife.

If you have already given away your virginity, choose Secondary Virginity. This means that you are choosing to regain your purity—that precious virginity of your inner self.

Whatever you do, don't give up on yourself and fall into the trap of believing "I'm not worth anything. Nobody would ever want me."

That is not true! Plenty of people—millions in fact—are in the same boat as you are. They are looking for someone to love and someone to love them. Some of the happiest marriages on the face of this earth result when the right, modest girl has met the right, clean young man.

TO SUMMARIZE...

Choosing to keep your purity is like choosing to wait until Christmas to open your presents. You don't lose anything by it. Your joy is greater because you waited until the right time.

Whether you are choosing to keep your virginity or choosing Secondary Virginity, here is a way to reinforce your decision. Get a tiny gold key. Let it represent the key to your heart and to your body. Keep it for the one you will marry. Give it to him on your wedding night.

Chapter 15

JUST FOR GUYS

JUST FOR

Let's face it. It's not easy for a young man to live a clean life in the world today. It never has been easy, and it never will be.

It's true that you face more temptation than your father did, and a whole lot more than your grandfather ever faced. You may have a tough situation at home, or even with the guys you call your friends, but that's no excuse. Others have come through, and you can too. here are some suggestions to help you:

Choose abstinence. Stay out of bed until you are married. Some day you will be glad you did. The future you save is your own.

A few years ago, the advocates of so-called "free sex" were saying, "There's nothing to be afraid of." They don't say that now. The sexually transmitted diseases have changed that. Even the "swingers" are disillusioned with free sex and terrified of getting AIDS or some of the other STDs.

Learn real love. Real love is caring enough about someone that you want what is best for that person. You are willing to sacrifice for the good of that person.

It's easy to deceive ourselves. The guy who says to a girl, "I love you and I want you to prove your love for me," may think that he really loves the girl. But what he's really saying is, "I love myself and I want to use you." That's backwards. We are supposed to love people and use things, not love things and use people.

Too many guys play around with girls and deceive them to get what they want. Don't be like them. Guys, please be careful with girls. Be honest with them. Don't build up false hopes. Don't tell a girl that you love her unless you really do love her with the right kind of love.

Sex before marriage causes all kinds of emotional problems. When the break-up comes, it's a lot tougher on the girls than on the guys. It's not something you want on your conscience—that you caused someone else to have deep emotional problems. At a high school assembly program, a well-known speaker was asked, "What do you regret most about your high school days?" Instantly he replied, "The thing I regret most about that time in my life is that I single-handedly destroyed a girl."

Learning unselfish love is laying the foundation for a happy marriage. Two people, each going their own way and making selfish choices, simply cannot make a go of a marriage.

Treat girls with respect. Many girls—even the popular, out-going ones—are basically insecure. They need friends to encourage them and build them up. They especially need friends of the opposite sex who show by their actions that they respect them.

Get to know some girls. Be a friend to them. Treat them as you would like a guy to treat your sister. When you are going too far, a girl should tell you no. But she shouldn't have to keep telling you no.

You don't have to act like Rambo to impress the girls. What really impresses girls is the combination of strength and gentleness in a guy. Macho guys can be thoughtful. Macho guys can be courteous. Macho guys can be unselfish. Macho guys can be strong and clean.

Make it a point to get to know your girl as she really is. Most dates are too superficial. Any girl can be sweet around the house when she's trying to impress her boyfriend. Likewise, any guy can act like a gentleman when he's trying to impress the girl's family. But most of life is lived in the ordinary way.

Learn to enjoy the company of girls without the physical. Courtesy is in, and bad manners are out. Treat your girl like a queen and she will act like one.

Practice the Golden Rule. The Golden Rule says, "Do unto others as you would have them do unto you." That's a good rule for guys in their dating relationships. Treat a girl like you want some guy to treat the girl you will marry some day. Do not give or take that which may some day rightfully belong to another person.

Tom dated Mary for some time. They discovered that they were not meant for each other, so they began dating others. Even though they were no longer dating, Tom became a real friend to Mary and she appreciated and respected him for it. Later, Mary started dating Bob. Tom became Bob's friend also. In time Bob and Mary became engaged. When they made their wedding plans, both of them wanted Tom to be in their wedding. It was a happy occasion for all three because Tom had treated Mary with respect and had nothing to be ashamed of. That's the way it ought to be.

Some guys have some weird ideas on this subject. They think it's fine for them to fool around and try to seduce every girl they go out with. But then, when they are ready to "settle down and marry," they want a pure girl— not one who has been pawed over by a lot of guys. Read this letter to Ann Landers:

When are girls going to get smart and demand the same standard of virtue that the boys demand of them? The guy who wants to play around with tramps while he's dating and then expects a good girl when he's "ready for something important like marriage" ought to be sent to the bargain basement right along with the girls he helped to put there.

I've been talking this way for a long time, Ann. When I was in high school, girls told me that I'd never find a boy with standards that high. But I found him and married him, and I'll wager that he is more manly than those creeps who had so much "proving" to do before marriage.

I'm sure I didn't get the only good guy in the world. There must be others left. Happy hunting, girls.

Mrs. Lucky [1]

Guard your thought life. A rule concerning computers is GIGO—"garbage in—garbage out." The same is true of your mind. If you put garbage into your mind, you will get garbage out.

Avoid pornographic trash like a plague. You become what you read. If you allow that filthy stuff into your mind, you will be entertaining filthy thoughts and you will soon be doing filthy things.

Discipline yourself. You will never amount to much in life if you don't learn to discipline yourself. Discipline means doing what you ought to do, when you ought to do it, whether you feel like it or not.

A young college fellow was explaining to his professor why he skipped his last class. He said, "I just didn't feel like it." The professor roared back, "Young man, did it ever occur to you that most of the work done in this world is done by people who don't feel like it?"

Guys that excel in the sports know what discipline is. They are not doing drugs, drinking and running around half the night. They know that winning involves a price tag and they're willing to pay that price. They are not slaves to their passions and desires. They make their bodies do what they choose for them to do.

You may or may not be on a sports team, but make it a point to get some hard exercise every day. You will feel better and find it easier to control your desire for sex. Exercise will burn up your excess energy and relieve the tension you feel at home. A guy who has had two hours of football or basketball practice or jogged five miles is not likely to be riding around in the evening looking for a girl.

Be a man of your word. Real men are always men of their word. Far too many people are careless about their word. Cason Callaway, founder of Callaway Gardens, said, "I know men who, if they told me casually, 'I will write you a letter about that tomorrow,' and I didn't receive the letter, I would send flowers. I would know that they were dead."

The world is full of undependable people—people who cannot be counted on. They make promises but their word is not worth a plug nickel. Being dependable means keeping your word. Do you mean what you say? Do you keep your word?

WHAT SEPARATES THE MEN FROM THE BOYS

The thing that separates the men from the boys is something called maturity. Maturity means that you are able to see the big picture and make decisions based on it. It's looking beyond the fun-for-the-moment way of living to your long future and choosing the course of action that will pay off later.

Immaturity says, "I want it now." Maturity says, "I will wait for the right time and the right circumstances." Immaturity says, "I want my own way." Maturity says, "I will practice the Golden Rule and consider the other person." When the going gets tough, immaturity says, "I quit!" Maturity says, "When the going gets tough, the tough get going."

Puffing on a cigarette doesn't turn a boy into a man. Having sex with a girl won't make you a man. Cruising and boozing won't do it either. And no amount of drugs can turn a wimp into a man. If you become a man, you're going to have to earn it the old fashioned way—by working for it.

The real macho guy is the one who has enough guts and enough self-respect to do what's right even if he's the only one doing it. He's the guy who stands tall in a world contaminated with the "everybody's doing it" philosophy.

"THIS GUY REALLY LOVES ME!"

Treat all girls with respect, but when you meet the girl that you think might be the one for you, guard that relationship as you would guard a priceless treasure. There's hardly anything more wonderful in this world than the love of a pure woman who happens to be your wife. You can't expect that unless you keep yourself and your relationships pure. That means taking your share of the responsibility and not putting it all on the girl.

Too many guys just want to do what gives them a good feeling. Too many want to play around with sex but they are not willing to take responsibility for their actions. Almost any guy can father a child, but it takes a man to be a good husband and a good father to a child. Sex is serious business. It brings babies into the world and babies have tremendous needs. Most of all, they need two parents to provide for their material needs and to give them love and guidance.

One who is happily married tells how her husband proved that his love was real during their engagement:

My husband and I dated for three and one-half years and were engaged during the last of those years. One night during that time we allowed our feelings to get overheated and almost did the proverbial "it."

In the heat of the situation, my husband stopped his actions and said, "I wouldn't do that to you."

His statement hit me right between the eyes and made me think to myself, "Gosh, this guy really loves me!" When all systems were saying, "Go for it," he got himself back under control and thought of me first.

It said to me that this guy was terrific husband material because he could love me over himself. It said he was also good father material because, if he could love me over himself, he could love our children over himself.

We've been married for 15 years, and have three children, and enjoy intercourse more and more each

138

year because love and intercourse are directly related in marriage. The deeper our love for each other grows—the sharing of our inner lives—the more enjoyable our intercourse becomes.[2]

TO SUMMARIZE...

It doesn't take much of a guy to be selfish, immoral and immature. What separates the men from the boys is something called maturity—being able to see the big picture and act accordingly. Macho guys can be unselfish. Macho guys can be strong and clean.

"This guy really loves me!"

NOTES

CHAPTER 2
1. Martyn Grotjohn, *Family Weekly*, 17 November 1974.
2. Patricia McGerr, *Woman's Day*, November 1965.

CHAPTER 3
1. Mary Ann Visker, *Group Members Only,* June-August 1988, p. 5.
2. *Youthwalk,* May 1988, p. 10.
3. James C. Dobson, *Hide or Seek* (Old Tappan, NJ: Fleming H. Revell, a division of Baker Book House, 1974) pp. 116,117.

CHAPTER 4
1. Ann Landers, *Ann Landers Talks to Teenagers About Sex* (Englewood Cliffs, NJ: Prentice-Hall, Inc., 1963) p. 37.
2. Center for Disease Control Report.
3. *Quick Facts on "Safe Sex,"* (Colorado Springs, CO: Focus on the Family, 1992) p. 4.
4. Ibid, p. 4.
5. Rubie Senie, Center for Disease Control.
6. Nicole Wise, *STRAIGHT TALK* (Emmaus, PA: Rodale Press, 1991) Vol. 1, No. 2, p. 3.
7. *Quick Facts on "Safe Sex,"* p. 4.
8. Ibid, p. 4.
9. Ibid, p. 4.
10. John Dietrich, *AIDS: Facts vs. Fiction* (Colorado Springs, CO: Focus on the Family, 1982) p. 4.
11. *Quick Facts on "Safe Sex,"* p. 4.
12. Suggested by Dr. James Dobson.
13. Theresa Crenshaw, from remarks made at the National Conference on HIV, Washington, D.C., November 15-18, 1991
14. *STRAIGHT TALK.*
15. *AIDS: Facts vs. Fiction,* p. 12.
16. Nolan Ryan (and Jerry Jenkins), *Miracle Man* (Waco, TX: Word Publishing, 1992).

CHAPTER 5
1. January '92 Center for Disease Control Survey.
2. Ann Landers, *Ann Landers Talks to Teenagers About Sex* (Englewood Cliffs, NJ: Prentice-Hall, Inc., 1963) pp. 118, 119.
3. Ann Landers.
4. Dear Abby.
5. Source Unknown.
6. Ann Landers.
7. National Adolescent Student Health Survey, as quoted in *USA Today.*
8. *USA Today*, 24 July 1992.

CHAPTER 7

1. *Time* Magazine, 26 July 1993.
2. Jay Strack, *Drugs and Drinking,* (Nashville, TN: Thomas Nelson Inc., 1985) p. 18.

CHAPTER 8

1. *National Geographic,* February 1992, p. 19.
2. Ibid, p. 37.

CHAPTER 10

1. "Stan Marsee's Smokeless Death" *Reader's Digest,* October 1985.

CHAPTER 12

1. *Guideposts* Magazine Inc.

CHAPTER 14

1. Ruth Vaughn, *To Be a Girl, To Be a Woman* (Old Tappan, NJ: Fleming H. Revell, a division of Baker Book House, 1983).
2. Elisabeth Elliot, *Passion and Purity,* (Old Tappan, NJ: Fleming H. Revell, a division of Baker Book House, 1984).

CHAPTER 15

1. Ann Landers, *Ann Landers Talks to Teenagers About Sex* (Englewood Cliffs, NJ: Prentice-Hall, Inc., 1963) p. 115.
2. Karen Poza, *Saying No, the Way to Grow* (Toronto, Canada: Life Cycle Books, 1982) pp. 29, 30.

Peer Pressure

Find out how to feel good about yourself. Learn how to take control of your life. You can be a winner! Learn how. Some chapter titles:

- I Want to Belong!
- I'm Somebody!
- How to Say NO (Nicely)
- How to be a Winner

144 pages. $8.95

Understanding Your Sex Drive

This book is a must for teens! You've got to know the five "laws" of guy-girl relationships. Chapter titles include:

- What is the Sex Drive?
- The Priceless Gift
- The Five "Laws" of Guy-Girl Relationships
- The Best Sex

96 pages. $7.95

Love and Dating

The book that tells you what real love is. Learn how to recognize the various kinds of false love. Some chapter titles:

- What is Real Love?
- How to Rate With Your Date
- How Far is "Too Far"?
- Three Kinds of Love

96 pages. $7.95

ORDER FORM

	QUANTITY	PRICE	TOTAL
LOVE AND DATING			
Paperback Item #BD-117		7.95	
Hardback Item #BD-121		12.95	
UNDERSTANDING YOUR SEX DRIVE			
Paperback Item #BD-118		7.95	
Hardback Item #BD-122		12.95	
PEER PRESSURE			
Paperback Item #BD-119		8.95	
Hardback Item #BD-123		13.95	
3 BOOK SET			
Paperback Item #BD-120		20.00	
Hardback Item #BD-124		35.00	

SHIPPING:
$2.00/first book
$.75 each additional book
OUTSIDE USA: Add $3.00/book
Please pay in US funds.

Subtotal	
Shipping	
GA residents add 7% sales tax	
TOTAL	

Payment must accompany order

Make check or money order payable to:
MAILBOX CLUB BOOKS
For credit card orders call 1-800-488-5226
Fax: (912)245-8977 • E-Mail: mailboxclb@aol.com

MAIL TO   Please print your name and address on the mailing label below

MAILBOX CLUB BOOKS
404 Eager Road
Valdosta, GA 31602-1399

To: _____

_____

_____

_____